CAROLE I. WEST

Don't Wait

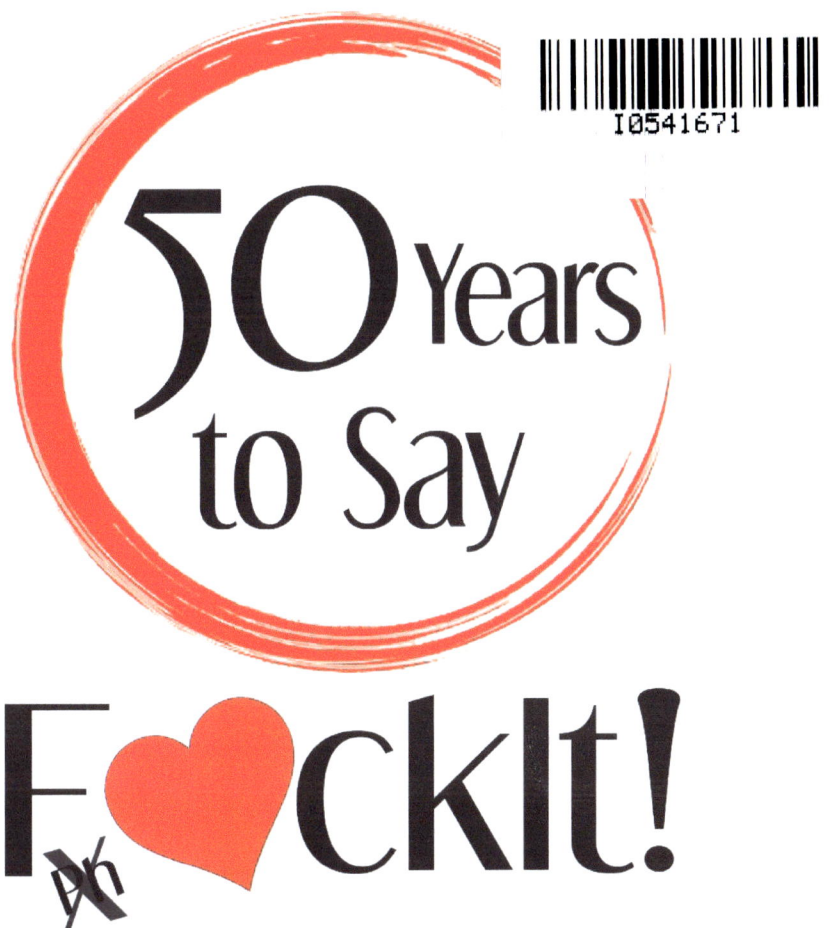

50 Years
to Say

F♥ckIt!

**Wisdom and lessons learned.
Learning to let sh*t go!**

Library of Congress Control Number: 2024922867
Orders by U.S. trade bookstores and wholesalers

ISBN: 979-8-9914117-7-6

Cover Design: Kasper Harris

Illustration Design: Jamal Grant and Kylie Grant

Original Editing: Laurie West
Final Editing: Veronica Miller: reddiamondediting5@yahoo.com

First Printed Edition: May 2025

Welcome to the Storm Publishing!

❤️ Gratitude ❤️

Before He formed me in the womb, He knew me. He saw me, He loved me, and He chose me. I am in awe of God's grace and thankful beyond words for the life He has given me, the challenges, the triumphs, the lessons, and the growth. Through it all, He has molded me into the woman I am called to be, and I will forever praise Him for His purpose in my life. ❤️

To my parents, Michael and Janet West, thank you for your profound love and unwavering support. You chose me and ensured I had a strong foundation to build my life upon. Thank you for being my first teachers in life, for giving me the freedom to explore the world on my own terms, for being a constant source of encouragement I've always needed and your belief in me that gave me the confidence to pursue my dreams. I am who I am because of you. ❤️

To my children, Laisha, Jamal, and Kylie, you are my heart and my motivation. Thank you for your patience during the times I stumbled, for your honesty when I needed perspective, for your encouragement when I felt uncertain, and most of all thank you for your love, which has carried me through so many moments. I know I haven't always gotten everything right, but I am so grateful for your grace and the ways you inspire me to keep growing and evolving. You are my greatest blessings, and I strive every day to be the mother you deserve. ❤️❤️❤️

To my siblings, extended family, and friends, you are the village that has nurtured me, cheered me on, and stood by me through every season of my life. Thank you for being a source of strength and joy, for celebrating my victories, and for supporting me in my struggles. Your love and encouragement have been a priceless gift. I am so blessed to have you in my corner. ❤️

To my Sorority Sisters of Delta Sigma Theta Sorority, Incorporated, thank you for the sisterhood that transcends time and space. You have given me friendship, accountability, shared purpose, and so many cherished memories. The values of our bond inspire me daily, and I am proud to be part of this incredible legacy of service, excellence, and love. ❤️

To my fellow HBCU alumni of the University of Arkansas at Pine Bluff, thank you for being an extended family of support and pride. The experiences we've shared and the connections we've built have enriched my life in countless ways. Thank you for uplifting me and reminding me of the power of community and collective strength. ❤️

To JD, my Soror and fellow alumnus, my fiercest critic and most loyal accountability partner, I love you and I thank you for the years of friendship. ❤️

To everyone who has played a role in my journey, please know that your impact is felt deeply. Each of you has shaped me in unique and meaningful ways, and for that, I will forever be grateful. ❤️

50 Years to F❤ckIt!

During my 50th birthday trip to Phuket, Thailand, I found myself standing on a deserted stretch of beach as the last rays of sunlight dipped below the horizon. The air was thick with the scent of salt and jasmine, and waves lapped gently at my feet. It was there, under the crimson sky, that an epiphany struck me, I am free to be me.

For years, I had carried the weight of expectations like a backpack I couldn't take off, whether they came from others or myself. But at that moment, I knew it was time to let go. Time to embrace a new chapter, guided not by outdated beliefs or past mistakes, but by authenticity and the deep desire to choose my own path.

For so long, I had been tethered to expectations that weren't my own – expectations that were handed down by others, by societal norms, and even by the unrelenting critic in my own mind.

Each role I played, each belief I clung to, weighed me down. But on that sunlit beach, I saw it for what it was: a story I didn't have to keep telling. It was time to rewrite the narrative. I realized I could let go – of outdated beliefs, past mistakes, and the parts of myself shaped by "should haves" rather than "wants." And as I let the waves carry those old stories away, I felt a sense of liberation I hadn't known was possible.

Turning 50 wasn't just another milestone – it was a gateway. A gateway to a life where I could choose to live authentically, unapologetically, and intentionally. In that moment of clarity, I understood that the world isn't just a vast expanse to explore; it's also a mirror reflecting the inner terrain we uncover when we dare to embrace who we are.

I no longer needed to chase perfection or acceptance. The freedom to make mistakes, to be imperfect, was not only liberating – it was necessary.

As I reflect on the twists and turns of my life, I see each chapter differently now. The mistakes, the heartbreaks, the triumphs – they weren't detours. They were lessons. Even the moments I once wanted to forget have become threads in the tapestry of my story.

My family history, once overlooked, now feels like an anchor, a foundation that shaped my identity. And the way our brains work – the thoughts and beliefs that mold our realities – has taken on a profound significance for me. It's fascinating to think about how early conditioning and societal pressures can dictate so many of our choices without us even realizing it.

Looking back, I see how pivotal my choices were, especially in relationships. The paths I chose were often fraught with challenges and unexpected turns, but they led to growth, to understanding, and to strength.

These lessons didn't come without a cost; every choice leaves an imprint, after all. But with time, and with the guidance of both faith and therapy – I've learned to see those imprints as evidence of a life lived fully.

Religion and therapy offered me the tools to step back from the chaos and see life from a higher vantage point. They gave me clarity when I felt lost, peace when I felt overwhelmed, and wisdom when I needed it most.

One of the greatest lessons I've learned is the power of letting go. Letting go of toxic habits, letting go of self-doubt, and most importantly, letting go of the need to be anyone other than who I am.

It's not easy to shed old layers, especially when they've been part of your identity for so long. But the freedom that comes with release is unparalleled. Letting go isn't just a decision; it's a declaration – a promise to myself that I will no longer carry what no longer serves me.

So, as I step into this next chapter, I do so with a light heart and open hands. The future is unwritten, and that's what makes it so exciting. Each blank page is an opportunity to choose joy, to choose authenticity, and to choose me.

And as a tribute to this transformative journey, I'll be using "ph" in place of the letter "f" throughout this book, honoring the trip to Phuket that sparked my awakening. A heart will replace the letter "u," symbolizing that **you** and **your heart** are central to everything you do, even in embracing imperfection by saying "fuck it." "PhckIt!"

So here I am, standing at the edge of the unknown, ready to write the next chapter with intention, courage, and freedom. If there's one thing I've learned, it's that life isn't about chasing an idea – it's about choosing yourself over and over again.

So here I am, ready to embrace the unknown, understanding that the choices I make from here on out will author my next chapters. And this time I'm choosing me, and I choose to be free.

PhckIt!

Table of Contents

Introduction

The Invisible Girl

For as long as I can remember, being adopted and biracial I've lived in the shadows of life, feeling invisible. I've spent my entire existence searching for something – aching, yearning, desperately awaiting its arrival.

Can you imagine that? The relentless pursuit of an unknown "something," a longing that drives you to the edge, only to face the bitter truth that what you thought was "it" never truly was.

As an eternal optimist, I know the ride all too well. It's a ph♥cking roller coaster ride. The highs and lows. The hope. The heartache. The belief that when it finally comes, you'll recognize it, only to realize – once again – that it isn't what you were searching for.

It was January 2013, and I wrote the following:

Is this really what my life is about? Day in and day out, barely making it into work because I am tired of the emotional and professional abuse from others, only to make it home some 10 hours later, to be ushered into continuing to serve the needs of others. Is this what I was called for? To take care of everyone else's needs.

God…what is my purpose? Why did you put me on this earth? What is it that you are trying to get out of me? Where am I supposed to go? Who am I supposed to be? I can't imagine life continuing like this, day after day of the same mundane thing.

Life is supposed to be about living. Experiencing new things, helping others accomplish their goals, enjoying every waking moment you have.

So, why is it that I just sit back and feel like my life is slipping by?

Why is it that I find myself living for everyone else and not living for myself?

At what point will I find the solution to what it is that I have been waiting for…looking for?

When am I going to find confidence and the conviction to know that what I am doing daily is what it is that you have called me to do?

I know I am not normal.

I know that you did not call me to be mediocre.

I know that you did not put me on this earth, allow me to have the experiences I had, to allow me to remain in a position of stagnation.

God, I need you! I need to know where you want me to go and when I need to be there.

Allow the Holy Spirit to guide me daily.

I am tired of trying to figure it all out in my head.

Allow me to surrender myself to you; to yield to the spirit and find the direction towards the path you want me to take.

I am a willing vessel

God. I just need you to speak clearly to me, so that I can understand what your direction to me is.

Show me how to be that virtuous woman you called me to be.

Eleven years before I started writing this book, that's exactly how I was feeling – lost, uncertain. Those were the thoughts I wrestled with, the prayers I sent to God: Purpose, Direction, Guidance,

Wisdom.

For years, I've wandered, like Moses, through an endless wilderness, clinging to the faith that The Almighty has a plan for me. I may not understand it yet, but I trust it's there. I was taught that if I place my trust in Him, He will create a way where there seems to be no way. And let me tell you this: He always has.

Don't Wait 50 Years to Say Ph❤cklt! isn't just part of my story – it's the essence of it. Once an invisible girl, I grew into a woman destined for greatness, but not without being forged in the fire of struggle, pain, and tragedy. Every hardship has shaped me into who I am today, leaving its mark like a chisel carving away at stone, revealing the truth beneath.

And here's the thing: I wasn't designed to fit in. From the beginning, my path wasn't meant to follow the crowd or conform to anyone else's vision of who I should be. My journey has been about discovering the power of standing apart, of being unapologetically myself.

If you're anything like me, there have been moments in your life when you've wanted to scream "Ph❤cklt!" – Ph❤cklt! all. The exhaustion, the expectations, the never-ending demands. As women, as mothers, we often feel like the weight of the world rests solely on our shoulders. It doesn't – but it feels like it does. We pour so much of ourselves into solving everyone else's problems that we forget to pause and ask: What about me?

This book is about reclaiming your power – about finding the courage to say "Ph❤ck Fear!" and "Ph❤ck Adversity!" Don't let fear confine you to the sidelines of your own story. Don't let life's challenges define your limits. The enemy would have you believe that you're restricted, that your current circumstances are the boundaries of your future. But that's a lie. You are powerful, limitless, and capable of greatness.

Like an olive, you will be refined by the crushing. Let this book remind you that the breaking isn't your end—it's your transformation. Harness the strength within you, strive unapologetically for what your heart desires, and embrace the journey ahead. The time to choose yourself is now.

How I arrived at Ph❤cklt!

For the past few years, I've been on a transformational journey of rediscovering who I am, what I like, what I don't like, and where I'm headed in the next chapters of my life. Some call it a "midlife crisis". Some may experience this transformation and rediscovery of self when they become empty nesters – gaining more time to focus on self and life purpose rather than kids.

The path of my transformation began with a conversation with my brother Dave. Dave's job allowed him to work remotely from anywhere in the world, though he didn't go further than North America. A few years ago, while he was spending a month in Mexico – yes, an entire month! He sent me this beautiful photo of the turquoise blue water and his view from the condo he was renting.

That ph❤cker knew it would make me jealous as my happy place has always been somewhere sunny with the sun's rays beaming down on my body and my feet in the sand. I cherish the spectacular views of turquoise waters (not that dirty river or lake water) and the sound of the ocean waves crashing on the shore. I immediately picked up the phone to share my jealousy of him and the heightened state of discontentment I was feeling in my own life.

We were daydreaming about vacationing, and the various places we would rather be, and my brother brought up Phuket (Poo-ket), Thailand. He told me to pull it up on the map, and when I finally found it, I said, "fuck it?" We both giggled because I pronounced Phuket without considering the actual pronunciation. After the back-and-forth bantering and giggling with my brother, I made a declaration that day. One day, I am going to Phuket!

In 2023, some of my friends were having grand parties and celebrations for their milestone 50th birthdays. That fall, I started to wonder what I should do for my milestone event. I knew I had to do something significant because at least two of my previous milestone birthdays were not celebrated in the typical and traditional way. I was pregnant during both my 16th and 21st birthdays – not ideal, but chapters in my story nonetheless.

I knew I didn't want to have a party, because I don't always enjoy being around other people. I may have a passion for investing in the development of others, but if you really know who I am, I am a bit of a loner. I enjoy basking in my alone time. In my previous jobs, I would have long drives of four to five hours between work locations, and I would often spend the entire drive in silence. I also enjoy listening to jazz music, the kind without words, because it allows me to focus on the thoughts in my mind, and music transports me to wherever I want to be.

As I was reflecting on what I should do to celebrate my 50th birthday, I thought if I celebrated myself and all the things I have overcome and accomplished in this life, I must do something special. Despite being in debt, I thought if You Only Live Once (YOLO) then somehow, someway, I am going to Phuket!

I knew the trip would be expensive, as flights from the US to

Thailand can cost an average of $1500 per person. I knew it was a tall ask for any of my friends to join me, especially because the trip was to solely celebrate me. Who has that kind of money to casually invest in a girlfriend's birthday? Not too many.

When my girlfriend of 30 years heard where I wanted to go, she immediately said, "I will go with you!" JP had the disposable income, time, and resources to join me on this trip of a lifetime. Ph❤ck yeah! I decided that I was going to leverage my mispronunciation of Phuket and used the slogan: Ph❤ckIt! I'm 50. Let the planning begin!

I have so much appreciation for JP. When I met her, I was just a few years out of college, lost and unclear on how to navigate my career. She was a few years older than me and established in her career, with a passion for helping others. Instantaneously, we clicked! JP poured into me and helped me land my first executive level role at the age of 26.

JP started out as my very first mentor. Over the years we became colleagues and followed one another as we both moved to new companies. More importantly, she became my friend. JP is a root in my life and part of my inner circle. She provides that sisterhood bond and has helped me through the many storms of life, weathering all types of chaos. Through it all our friendship has remained steadfast. I can share anything with her and despite the distance or time, when we connect, it's as if we haven't missed a moment.

During the planning for the trip, she was so flexible, willing to do whatever I wanted to do on this adventure. JP allowed me to create our itinerary and supported everything I wanted to do. She said she just wanted to be there with and for me on my journey. A rare friend indeed. ❤

Life had been life'ing and there were plenty of distractions leading up to this trip. When the time came, I was so ready to escape my present environment: a time when there was chaos on all fronts and discontentment all around. Even getting to the airport that evening was stressful. We spent hours navigating the LA traffic, only to be brought to a standstill for what seemed like hours at the entrance of the airport. Escapism was the only thing in the forefront of my mind.

I will spare you the details of the exhausting flight (young children sat directly behind me the entire time), but I will share one lesson learned: Do NOT sit in a window seat for a 17-and-a-half-hour flight! Especially if you are of a certain age and need to use the restroom often!

We intentionally planned a long layover in Singapore to explore the city before boarding our flight to Bangkok. We quickly hopped in a cab and the adventures began. We spent a few days in Bangkok and a few days in Krabi and ended our adventures in Phuket. As a woman who loves adventure and seeing new things, I packed our agenda with sightseeing, boat rides, feeding the elephants, and visiting the temples. I didn't realize until the last day that I didn't plan any time to spend with myself. Time to just sit, explore my thoughts and plans for life, until that very moment, waiting for the sunset, on the last full day of our vacation.

As I was relaxing in the pool, eagerly awaiting one of the most beautiful sunsets I have ever seen, I felt an unrelenting need to get my phone. I had been watching this couple to the right of me. They were not interacting at all. Both were scrolling on their phones for what seemed like eternity. While other couples engaged in hand holding and talking with one another, enjoying the tropical beauty that encapsulated us all. They were what appeared to be obsessed with their phones, completely ignoring one another. I needed to capture my thoughts and the images at that very moment.

In the few minutes it took for the sun to fully set, the sun transformed from a bright and shiny yellow to a bright orange and miraculously it encompassed yellow, orange, and red as it set on the western coast of Phuket. The camera on my cell phone could never do it justice.

This was the time for me to begin writing about my journey.

I didn't want to lose this moment. I didn't want to miss the lesson I was supposed to learn in this moment. I grabbed my phone to not only capture the sunset but to also capture a reminder of the couple in the daybed below.

It came as no surprise to me that it proved to be watching that couple that prompted me to grab my phone and begin writing. I was so easily distracted by their engrossment in their phones that I began reflecting on my own relationship and how we interact together.

I thought to myself, "If my significant other was here with me, that would be us. That is us. And that is NOT what I want." Our choices have the tendency to bring us to exactly where we are in life.

As thoughts raced through my mind, I was reminded of both lessons learned and lessons taught throughout my professional career.

In one of the leadership classes I teach, I ask participants the following question:

Does all activity lead to results?

The audience typically bursts out with varying responses, as if the question is a trick question. There is also a bit of hesitation in standing firmly on their answers. After a few seconds of pause I happily shared with the class that the answer is *yes*.

All activity and actions lead to a result or reaction but is it the result or reaction we hoped for? Most people make a conscious and deliberate effort to engage in certain activities but fail to consider the consequences or stop and consider the after effect.

> # All activity leads to results, but is it the results you are hoping for?

My actions led me to a place that I did not want to be. I am responsible for the choices I make and if I want something different, I will have to make a different choice.

For a variety of reasons, I have held onto an internal perception of rejection for most of my life. I've learned that if a person carries the perception of rejection, that will become a projection into what we expect to receive and experience in life. This perception I held perpetuated limitless boundaries and poor choices in relationships. At this stage in my life, I am saying Ph♥ckIt! to the perception of rejection and embracing the woman I am becoming.

I've been searching for something magical my entire life. I want what I have never had. I want a relationship with someone that includes hand holding, laughter, deep thought-provoking conversations, not this technology enabled bullshit that has consumed every adult and child. I want a relationship that embodies love, respect, exploration, and damn it, fun. I deserve that. Ph❤ckIt! We all deserve that.

My journey of transformation and rediscovery has empowered me to embrace my Ph❤ckIt! phase.

In my 50 years on this earth, I've been a parent for 35. For a mere 15 years, I was not responsible for the care and wellbeing of another human. I lived my life with the soul of another attached to me, intertwined in my heart, controlling my decisions, my focus, and MY life.

Getting pregnant at 15, I said Ph❤ckIt! and took on the world. I thought I was ready. I thought I was grown, and no one could tell me what to do, how to do it, or even when to do it. As ready as I thought I was, I wasn't. When is a person ever ready to take on what this ph❤cked up world is waiting to unleash?

Now that I've reached my 50's, I'm renewing my Ph❤ckIt! attitude. Embracing the same mentality as my fifteen-year-old self, but with wisdom. **These words of wisdom are my gift to you**.

Words to help you better embrace this ph❤cked up world and say Ph❤ckIt! to retreating due to obstacles or barriers that get in the way of your dreams.

Saying Ph❤ckIt! to unfulfilling careers that cause more stress and mental health issues than financial rewards or simply saying Ph❤ckIt! to bad relationships, letting them go, and moving on in your life's journey.

Throughout this book, I will share lessons learned based upon the actions I took and choices I made. In many of my actions and choices, I failed to assess the consequences of my choices and ended up with results I was not expecting, producing lessons learned. The purpose of this book is for others to learn from my experiences and from my life.

- I felt rejected and abandoned as a little girl, so I sought comfort in the arms of men.

  ○ I felt alone navigating life, so I said Ph❤ckIt! and tried to raise myself.

  ○ I ended up raising babies, as a baby.

- My actions and choices perpetuated generational curses, so I am deliberate and intentional when considering my choices moving forward.

  ○ I didn't like the belief systems that were instilled in me, so I ventured out to discover a new foundation and built a new belief system in Christ.

  ○ I continue to make mistakes along the way, but I seek wisdom from people who have navigated the terrain ahead of me.

- I was born to stand out. I am a Black maverick.

  ○ Racism, classism, White privilege and fragility are all real.

  ○ Just because you can, doesn't mean you should.

  ○ I learned to edit myself. Not everything you want to say must be said.

  ○ You don't have to pick up anyone else's shit, you have your own to deal with.

  ○ It's just a job.

- Life gets to life'ing for all of us.

  ○ Leverage clinical, spiritual, and community resources

to assist in building a foundation of support for your journey in life.

- ° There are resources out there that are specifically designed to help you.

- You were born on purpose, for a purpose.

We do not control when we are born, and for the most part, we surely do not control when we die. The only thing we are responsible for are the choices we make and how we live that dash in-between. What will you do with your dash? Time waits for no one. All actions have outcomes AND consequences.

The choices you make will bring you to exactly where you are in life. Now is your time to seek healing and take back your power. Redefine your future and let your past fuel you.

In order for me to fully understand why I make the choices I do, I had to go back to my roots. I needed to understand how my upbringing laid the foundation for my belief system.

Roots

R oots are a tree's foundation. Tree roots, whether strong and deeply embedded in the soil or broad and interwoven, play a crucial role in establishing an anchor system for the developing trunk, branches, and leaves. Roots also absorb nutrients and water, which are essential for a tree's growth. The primary function is to provide stability, a vital role in the tree's growth, prosperity, and survival.

Just as roots are an anchor for a tree, parents serve as the roots to the foundational support for their children. Parents provide the nurturing and guidance necessary for the children to feel grounded in life.

Parents nourish their children with not only physical care but also emotional, intellectual, and moral guidance, allowing the child to grow and develop in a healthy, balanced way.

Roots are responsible for the overall health of a tree, much like how parents influence the well-being of their child. Even though roots are not always visible, they are crucial to the tree's survival, much like the often unseen but deeply impactful role parents play in shaping a child's character, values, and sense of self. As the tree grows, its roots continue to support it, just as parents continue to offer love and wisdom, helping their child navigate life as they mature and face new challenges.

We have rooted relationships, often with family members or close friends or an intimate partner. These relationships are necessary for survival and provide the support required to grow. Who is part of your roots system may change over time, but more than likely, will remain with you for a lifetime. We build our belief systems from the relationships built with our roots.

The foundation of humanity began with the relationship between a man and a woman. In the biblical sense, creation began with the inception of life within a woman's womb. The purpose for the intimate act of sex is to produce a child. And let's be honest with one another, sex works whether a relationship exists or not.

There are couples who are deliberate and intentional when having sex, and they have intentions of creating a life, but this is not always the case. I may even venture to say that this is often NOT the case. A byproduct of sex is a whole lotta pleasure, that sometimes produces a child.

Sex Works!

And if the people having sex aren't ready for the outcome, parenting a child can be a huge undertaking. Relationship commitments are there to engage in sex, but that commitment doesn't always extend beyond the act of intimacy. There is a saying, *mama's baby, daddy's maybe*. There are far more people focused on immediate self-gratification than the consequences and/or outcomes from our actions. I was the byproduct of these self-indulgent decisions and let me tell you, sex *works*.

Complex issues come into play when partners aren't on the same page about what to do in the case of pregnancy. Parenting a child can be a huge undertaking, as there is a big difference between having a baby and raising one. The responsibility to raise a child can fall on both parents, one parent, adoptive or foster parents, grandparents, or even siblings – especially when there's an unexpected pregnancy.

I once heard an analogy comparing relationships and people to the parts of a tree. A tree is first established by the planting of a seed, followed by obtaining nutrients from its surrounding environment through the roots (family), and forming branches (friends) and leaves (acquaintances). Relationships are a necessary component for human life. Our relationships are like components of a tree.

Whether deep and personal or merely superficial, relationships are essential. Relationships help us in developing our foundation, our belief system, and our values. People come and people go. There are a few people who walk side by side with you for the entire duration of your life.

There are three types of people in our lives: those who last a lifetime (roots); those you may lose touch with, but you can always come back to (branches); and those who are seasonal and temporary (leaves).

So, remember these lessons, these sentiments, when choosing who will walk beside you on your journey through life.

A Foundation of Freedom

My Roots

The journey of transformation required me to slow down and examine my root system, to fully understand what makes me who I am. I had been rushing through life, navigating the dynamics of parenthood, career, and relationships, that I didn't realize the impact of my decisions.

Biologically, I am the offspring of selfish biological parents. They were committed to engaging in sexual pleasure without fully considering the consequences of their choices in the moment of ecstasy. I was adopted into an environment, consisting of well-intended White parents who failed to understand the implicit challenges of being Black in America. I was a Black child being raised by White parents. In a house with five kids, three were adopted (and Black), and two were biological (White).

Growing up in the '70's, parents gave their children the freedom and independence to explore their communities and surroundings with little structure, and my adoptive parents were no exception. I grew up on Jones Street, a middle-class White neighborhood in Omaha, where residents rarely locked the front door. As the youngest of five, I played in the neighborhood for hours, coming home only when I was hungry or tired. I don't recall a set time for dinner and my meals typically consisted of Spaghetti O's, cereal, or Totino's pizzas. The unlocked front door created an atmosphere of openness and accessibility for all.

We were latch key kids. We had so much freedom. We either snuck out of the house – or just walked out the front door quietly. We had house parties while our parents were at parties of their own. We threw toilet paper in the trees, egged cars and houses, and I am pretty sure all of us stole our parents' cars at least once.

We were free and independent kids, and our parents were busy focused on adulting. Their focus was everywhere other than us. There was just an occasional guardrail my parents erected when instilling boundaries and expectations of how we were to behave.

My mother was a workaholic, keenly focused on her career, her impact on the community and the lives of others. As a human resource professional, I often share my experiences of being raised in what I would call a "United Nations" household when questions arise surrounding my diversity, equity, and inclusion experience.

My mother was passionate about embracing foreign exchange students and welcoming them into our home. I often share that this experience is like being raised in a "United Nations" type household – everyone is welcome. She brought in students from Afghanistan, Africa, Australia, Bangladesh, China, Germany, India, Nepal, just to name a few. I woke up with the smell of curry cooking in the kitchen and even recall celebrating Hanukkah a few times, though we weren't Jewish.

My father was very involved in our extracurricular activities. He coached our sports and supported us in having friends over for sleepovers and gatherings. He taught me how to drive a manual transmission at the age of 10! He recently recalled a time when he let me drive one day on my paper route. Turns out, my paper route just so happened to be the same route my mother walked home from work every day. When she saw me driving and him running the papers to the porch, she let him have it! We still laugh about that to this day.

While each parent played a role in my development, neither were deliberate or intentional in developing my internal belief systems, self-esteem, or values.

I began exploring intimate relationships at a very early age. There was so much missing on the inside of me. I was a broken little girl, looking for something I had yet to understand. I didn't know what I was looking for, but the boys sure were cute! Flirting at school with my crush was exciting.

I remember my first crush and the butterflies in my stomach whenever he crossed my mind. The nervousness I felt, wondering if he would call. What would I say? Does he like me back? Growing up, all we had was a home phone, with an extra-long cord we would take all over the house, making sure we didn't miss that call. Remember the boy band New Edition? *Mr. Telephone Man, there is something wrong with my line….* Sorry about that, I went back to the 80's for a moment.

The very loose standards in my house meant that by eighth grade, my boyfriends were allowed to come visit and were also allowed to spend the night. That's not a typo. In eighth grade, I was allowed to have my boyfriend spend the night, and sleep in the bedroom with me. As a parent, I couldn't imagine allowing a boy to spend the night at my home in my teenage daughter's room. My parents were too disengaged and unaware of how their lenient approach to parenting would shape my future.

I had a contentious and fractured relationship with my mother. Growing up in a predominately White neighborhood with White neighbors and White friends, I never really felt as if I fit in. I struggled with an identity crisis most of my adolescent years. I often felt like an outcast and invisible. I wanted to fit in. I wanted to feel like I belonged. No matter what environment I went into, I moved in like a chameleon, adapting and adjusting to fit in or at least trying to fit in.

When I was 11, my mother took me to a Black hair salon. I was tired of having nappy pig tails and wanted to look less childish. I don't remember what was told to the stylist, but I walked out of there with a short jheri curl. What in the entire hell was I going to do now? Not only was I blessed with a unibrow, but now I also had a short jheri curl and didn't feel cute or confident in my appearance. How was I going to fit in now?

In a state of panic, I figured I could do what friends did, so I got some hair mousse shook it up and placed a heaping pile of mousse in my hair. That didn't work! I still looked like a hot mess. I was navigating this hair journey alone, at least I felt like I was alone. That is when I learned that I had to ask questions and get answers from those who looked like me.

My parents didn't know what to do with my hair. It took a couple of trips to the salon and repetitive lessons on how to effectively apply the curl activator and sleep with that nasty ass plastic cap on my head. But I finally got it right.

My identity started coming into perspective for me after my early adventures in the Black salon. When I started 7th grade of middle school, I began to seek friends who looked like me. Of course, I still had my White neighborhood friends, but I was intentional on finding Black friends, in hopes that I would feel like I fit in.

Fitting in with my Black community was my goal, but it didn't happen immediately. I was criticized for my communication style and speech (dialect), some of my Black classmates asked me why I talked so "White"? I didn't know what that meant, I was just communicating and talking the only way I knew how. I continued to internalize the perception that I still didn't fit in with my neighborhood friends or family. In retrospect, I think it became more about the story I was telling myself, rather than how others *actually* treated me. There was that one time though when an immediate family member called me the "n" word. That stung me to my core.

The narrative I created about not fitting in continued to grow with an increasing need for freedom and independence. I was a teenager, so of course I didn't want to abide by rules. I wanted to break the rules and create new ones that fit just for me. This is where the complications with my mother began.

We had a lot of freedom as kids, so giving me rules/boundaries as a teen, I thought was counterproductive. I didn't think any rules applied to me. Resisting the implicit rules in our home, I chose to defy every rule and stand in conviction that I knew what was best for me.

I was in the midst of a full blown, ongoing identity crisis. There were so many phases I went through. I hung out with punkers, with shaved heads and bright colored hair. I was 10 when my dad taught me how to drive. When I was 12, I got caught sneaking out of the house, but only after my dad looked outside and realized his car had left the driveway. My mother rushed over to pick up my dad and they headed to my boyfriend's house.

There I was – busted! Sitting in the driver's seat of my dad's Ford Tempo with my boyfriend and my bestie (a local Politian's daughter) in the back seat at 3 o'clock in the morning.

I hung out with people older than me perpetuating my false impression of being "grown". By the time I was 15, I had been kicked out of multiple schools, was dating a gang member, sold drugs and was placed on probation. My parents were so frustrated with my misconduct, disrespect, and complete disregard for their imposed boundaries, they didn't know what to do. My parents were not perfect, but they didn't deserve the level of disrespect I displayed towards them growing up.

By the time I was 16, I had transitioned from being adopted to becoming a ward of the state, and eventually to an emancipated minor and mother of my first-born, Laisha. Regardless of the contentious and fractured relationship I had with my mother, she and my father chose me. For that, I am eternally grateful. ♥

In early 2023, my mother died. She suffered for more than five years after a life-altering stroke disrupted her international globetrotting. She travelled to more than 120 countries in her years of post-retirement. She often traveled to countries where she could connect with families of previously sponsored foreign exchange students that she housed over the years. Her journeys even provided her with the privilege and honor of meeting our former President Barak Obama's step-grandmother.

After my sister Jami spent the first few years helping our mother navigate her new life of assisted living facilities, medical appointments, and physical therapy, with little to no improvement in her ability to recover, I volunteered to move our mother near me. Then Covid-19 took over the world and my mother's recovery and quality of life began to decline even more.

She spent her final years often worried about money knowing how expensive it was for her to live in an assisted living facility. Every time I would visit her, she would say, "Okay, now how much money do I have left?" While she had saved and invested well throughout her life she didn't grow up with much money and often worried about whether she would have enough to provide until her end of time. She said she wanted to die around the age of 91 so she had quite a bit longer to live.

She wanted to go to Iceland, she wanted to continue to travel the world, but her physical and now mental limitations were taking a toll on her. My mother would ask if she would have enough money to keep on living the life she lived. In her final days, she recalled and started reminiscing on significant milestones and memories of her own life, especially her memories with siblings and parents where money and resources were scarce. Watching her those last few months and days as she withered away encouraged me to put my own life into greater perspective. Was I living a life I loved?

She died in February 2023 at the age of 82.

When my mother died, I didn't grieve much. I cried a little and felt somewhat sad, but more relieved that she was no longer suffering and bound in a life she didn't want to live. I found it difficult to conjure up emotions and feelings and I did what I typically do: that is press on and move forward. I watched others go into deep mourning and sadness and I couldn't help but wonder why I had a limited emotional response. Just as quickly as that thought entered my mind, it dissipated.

In my natural take charge attitude, I immediately began planning and coordinating her homegoing celebration. I wanted to make sure it was one to be remembered. I reflected upon my mother's life and how she lived. My mother spent her lifetime dash helping others. She not only chose my brothers and me through adoption, but she made it a point to invite scores of international exchange students into our home throughout the years.

I previously shared that my mother traveled to more than 120 countries in her lifetime. Planning her celebration of life had to reflect the cultural curiosity and adventurous global travels she very much enjoyed.

Laisha delivered a heartfelt eulogy at my mother's beloved Unitarian Church. She described how influential and special my mother was to her. From instilling the importance of education to the late-night discussions about politics, relationships, and just about anything under the sun. My mother was my Laisha's rock, her confidant, and best friend.

During her memorial service I learned so much about her effect on other people's lives and her impact on the community and the higher education system in Nebraska. As a child I didn't question or even try to understand what my parents did in their professional life. I just knew them to be my parents. My mother taught economics for more than 40 years at the local university and my father was in sales most of his professional life. My mother was dedicated and committed to provoking change for teachers and disrupting the educational systems to make them better for teachers and students alike. My mother enjoyed challenging the status quo, she was a maverick!

Following the services guests were invited downstairs to the fellowship hall to have a deeper look at my mother's global adventures. We had international cuisine to excite the tastebuds of the local and international guests. We had A Taste of India with my mother's favorite dishes, as well as Three Happiness Express, the local favorite right around the corner from our childhood home, and Okra African Grill.

We created visual displays showcasing her cultural treasures picked up along the way. Displays of Danish porcelain trinkets and Russian nesting dolls to handmade ceramic plates from Romania. Shot glasses from Ireland because Jamison was her favorite whiskey and wood sculptures from Africa. She even picked up a license plate from her trip to Cuba – before US citizens were allowed to travel there.

My mother said Ph❤ckIt! she wanted to travel the world and be free, to live life on her terms, and that she did. On the next page is a picture of my mother during a girls' trips to Mexico in 2015. She was always up for adventure!

The way my mother lived her life – with a passion for giving to others, a resolve to challenge societal norms, and a zest for adventure to explore the world – has been a strong influence on my foundation. My father's unconditional support and spiritual foundation allowed us to have a close and connected relationship over the years. I always joke that I am his favorite child.

The relationship I had with my parents established my foundational belief system. As I reflected on my foundation of freedom and autonomy, I had to learn more about how that has affected my belief system and the choices I make today.

Our Belief System

What is a belief system?

According to Nicole Rivera, Ed.D.[1], belief systems shape behavior. Beliefs are developed largely through social modeling and direct messages that we receive from our surroundings. A belief may develop over a long period of time or in a few moments if the message is delivered in a powerful manner. Beliefs are also developed based on our cultural perspectives, some of which are derived from family and institutional culture.

Parents, Listen Up!

> # Parents, Listen Up!
> # It is YOUR job to teach your child.

You are the primary influence when creating your child's belief system, based upon what you expose your child to. You must be deliberate and intentional in how you raise your child. It is YOUR job to teach your child. It is not the school system, a nanny, a grandparent, a coach, a daycare, a friend; it is YOUR job to raise your child.

Your child will be looking to you to instill a foundation of values and morals. What you pour into them will foster their sense of purpose and direction in life. You will show them cultural and family identity as well as emotional resilience. You are building their brains for decision making healthy relationship standards and critical thinking.

Instilling a strong belief system will shape character and foster a positive sense of self. A strong belief system acts as a moral compass, helping us to understand the difference between right and wrong and lays the foundation for our core values.

The foundation of freedom and loose standards in my home strengthened my resolve to build my own framework and belief system. As a child, I didn't know how to explain how I was feeling on the inside. I didn't know how to articulate what I needed, and my parents were busy with outside activities that by the time they tried to get involved, I was too far gone to listen to anything they had to say.

My belief system was riddled with the intrinsic feeling of being ignored, excluded, rejected, and unseen. I felt invisible and alone. I remember when I was 17 years old, in a conversation with my dad, I told him that I don't recall hearing the words "I love you" from my mother. He of course reassured me that she did, but I never felt her love.

When I became a mother, I was determined to be different. I wanted my children to feel wanted and loved, but I really didn't know what I was doing.

Most parents will break their neck to ensure their children have something for their birthday and for the holidays. Even if they are gifted presents from civic organizations or friends, we want to ensure our children feel included and recognized during those special events. Parents may even make a special meal, have a special family game night, or make a personalized card with loving and kind words.

When we allow our children to participate in a birthday party for one of their friends, we will often take them to the store to buy that friend a birthday gift. We typically will not want our children to show up to the party empty-handed and risk embarrassment. And we get mad when they tell us about these invitations at the last minute, because we must scramble to get everything in order before party time.

Don't forget about the first day of school. We will go ALL OUT to ensure our children have new outfits, a fresh haircut or style, and they must have the fresh kicks to wear on the first day of school.

As parents, we plan. And if we don't plan, we pivot and adjust quickly to ensure our children's needs and sometimes wants are met. If we spend all that time, energy, and money preparing for a birthday party or the first day of school, why don't we keep that level of focus, intention, energy, and time in building a solid belief system?

Building our children's belief system begins with understanding how to build our brains.

Brain Development

Most early childhood educators know this fun fact, and unless you've done research on how to best raise and develop your child's brain, you may not have known either, until now. Ninety percent of brain development happens before the age of 5 years old.

The brain is an extremely complex organ that receives information, processes it, and defines our responses. It controls what we think and feel – our memories, learning, and bodily responses. Everything we think and do is directly connected to our past brain development.

90% of brain development happens before the age of 5.

Review the following diagram to gain a better understanding of when and what part of the brain develops.

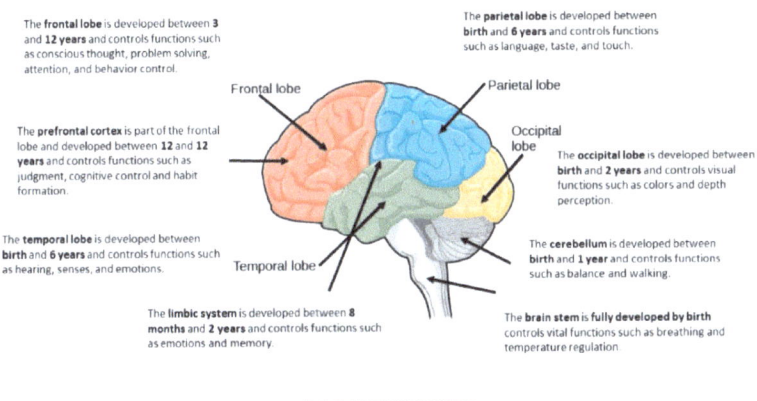

The **frontal lobe** is developed between **3** and **12 years** and controls functions such as conscious thought, problem solving, attention, and behavior control.

The **prefrontal cortex** is part of the frontal lobe and developed between **12 and 12 years** and controls functions such as judgment, cognitive control and habit formation.

The **temporal lobe** is developed between **birth** and **6 years** and controls functions such as hearing, senses, and emotions.

The **parietal lobe** is developed between **birth** and **6 years** and controls functions such as language, taste, and touch.

The **occipital lobe** is developed between **birth** and **2 years** and controls visual functions such as colors and depth perception.

The **cerebellum** is developed between **birth** and **1 year** and controls functions such as balance and walking.

The **limbic system** is developed between **8 months** and **2 years** and controls functions such as emotions and memory.

The **brain stem** is fully developed **by birth** controls vital functions such as breathing and temperature regulation

Frontal lobe

Parietal lobe

Occipital lobe

Temporal lobe

Let's start with the **brain stem**. The brainstem is **fully developed at birth** and controls vital functions necessary for survival, such as breathing, heart rate, and temperature regulation. These basic functions are crucial for a newborn's immediate adaptation to life outside the womb and allow the baby to maintain essential bodily functions autonomously. The brainstem's development ensures that the infant can breathe and regulate its body temperature without external support, laying the foundation for the baby's overall health and stability in the early stages of life.

The full development of the brainstem at birth allows for immediate, automatic responses to stimuli, helping the infant begin interacting with the environment and caregivers right away. This early development is key to the infant's survival and the initial phase of growth and adaptation.

The **cerebellum**, which develops between **birth and one year**, plays a crucial role in a baby's motor skills, particularly in balance and coordination. As it matures, the cerebellum helps the infant gain control over their body movements, allowing them to start developing basic physical skills like holding their head up, rolling over, and eventually sitting, crawling, and standing. This development is essential for a child's ability to navigate their environment and begin exploring the world around them.

The **occipital lobe**, which develops between **birth and two years** of age, is primarily responsible for processing visual information. As it matures, it enables babies to interpret and make sense of what they see, starting with basic visual functions like recognizing light and dark and progressing to more complex tasks such as identifying colors and understanding depth perception. This is a crucial phase in a baby's ability to visually explore their environment.

The **limbic system**, which develops **between 8 months and 2 years**, plays a key role in a baby's emotional and memory development. This area of the brain is responsible for **regulating emotions**, helping infants start to recognize and respond to feelings such as fear, joy, and frustration. As it matures, the limbic system allows babies to form emotional attachments to their caregivers, which is essential for building trust and security during early development.

The growth of the limbic system is vital for emotional bonding, social interaction, and the development of memory, laying the foundation for healthy emotional responses and the ability to recall important events and people in their lives.

The **temporal lobe**, which develops between **birth and six years** of age, is essential for processing sensory information, particularly related to hearing and emotions. As it matures, the temporal lobe helps babies interpret sounds and begin to develop language skills, enabling them to recognize familiar voices and respond to speech. This is a critical stage in the development of communication, as the brain starts to link sounds with meaning, laying the groundwork for language acquisition.

In addition to sensory processing, the **temporal lobe** plays a role in **regulating emotions**. It helps babies begin to understand and respond to their own emotional experiences, as well as those of others. The development of this area supports emotional regulation, empathy, and social interaction, which are crucial for building relationships and emotional intelligence. By the age of six, the temporal lobe's maturation enhances a child's ability to engage with their environment, communicate effectively, and manage their emotions, fostering both cognitive and social development.

The **parietal lobe**, which develops between **birth and six years**, plays a critical role in sensory processing and motor skills, particularly in language, taste, and touch. As it matures, it helps babies process sensory information, allowing them to understand and respond to different tastes and textures. This area of the brain also contributes to language development, supporting the baby's ability to recognize sounds, associate them with meaning, and eventually start speaking.

The **frontal lobe**, which develops between the ages of **3 and 12**, is crucial for higher-level cognitive functions such as conscious thought, problem-solving, attention, and **behavior regulation**. As it matures, the frontal lobe enables children to think more critically, plan, and make decisions. It also plays a significant role in **managing impulses** and controlling emotional responses, helping children to behave appropriately in different situations and **develop self-discipline**.

By the time a child reaches the age of 12, the frontal lobe's development helps them navigate social interactions, improve decision-making skills, and refine their ability to adapt to new challenges. This stage of brain development is essential for overall cognitive, emotional, and social growth, setting the foundation for more mature thought processes in adolescence and adulthood.

The **prefrontal cortex**, a key part of the frontal lobe, develops between the ages of **12 and 25** and is vital for higher-level cognitive functions such as judgment, decision-making, and cognitive control. As it matures, it enables children and adolescents to think more critically, evaluate situations, and make more reasoned decisions. The prefrontal cortex also plays a significant role in regulating emotions and impulses, helping individuals exercise self-control and focus on long-term goals rather than immediate desires. This is where we consider the pros and cons of a situation before acting or deciding.

Decision making is one of the last abilities to fully develop in the brain.

The prefrontal cortex is crucial for habit formation and adapting to new experiences. It allows individuals to develop routines, learn from past actions, and adjust behavior based on previous outcomes. This area of the brain is essential for refining executive functions, such as planning, problem-solving, and organizing, which are key for academic success, social interactions, and personal growth throughout adolescence and into adulthood.

Remember at 15, I said Ph♥ckIt! and was ready to take on the world? As a teenager, my emotions and decision-making ability were still developing and probably not at the same rate. Therefore, I frequently found myself being hijacked emotionally and responding out of emotions. Another interesting fact is that the brain doesn't fully develop and mature until a person is in their 20's.

The foundation of learning and brain development is set in place before the age of five, with early experiences having a significant impact on the brain's growth. During these early years, the brain forms crucial neural connections that influence cognitive, emotional, and physical development. This period is a critical window where a child's environment, relationships, and experiences shape the trajectory of their learning and abilities.

After the age of five, the brain continues to develop slowly but steadily for the next 20 years. This ongoing development helps refine cognitive skills, emotional regulation, and social behaviors. While development continues throughout adolescence and into adulthood, the early experiences truly lay the groundwork for a lifetime of learning and personal growth.

And there I was, learning all this critical information, after my three children were all past the age of 20! I was destined to replicate the environment in which I was raised.

Generational Curses

Let's keep it real. We all have those family secrets that we hope no one ever brings up at holiday dinners or get togethers. We all have generational curses in our families and some of us were born to break the curse – Like me. ❤️

Generational curses are repeated patterns of behavior passed down from generation to generation. Curses can look like addictions, mental health struggles, financial problems, or unhealthy relationship dynamics that seem to affect each generation in the same way. In a psychological sense, it is more about learned behaviors, trauma, or conditioning that get passed down, often unconsciously, from one generation to the next.

My unaddressed psychological trauma and conditioning unconsciously impacted my parenting style in many different ways. My trauma shaped how I interacted with my children, the expectations I placed on them, and how I did or did not respond to their emotional needs. Here's how my unaddressed trauma and conditioning manifested:

Emotional Reactivity: I was a ticking time bomb. My reactions and emotions were so unpredictable. I reacted out of anger and frustration towards my children when they misbehaved, or my interpretation of their behavior if I deemed it inappropriate. I never stopped to consider how my reaction would impact their emotional well-being. My responses were often triggered by my past emotional wounds. The tragedy is that by the time I learned to control my emotional and hyper critical responses, my children had already developed their own attachment style and coping skills.

Inconsistent Parenting: My parenting style shifted so frequently, what Laisha experienced as a child was different from what Jamal and Kylie experienced. I was extremely controlling and restrictive with Laisha and Jamal and by the time Kylie was growing up, I was so tired of trying to control everything, I became extremely lenient. That created confusion within my children. They didn't understand why I showed up differently for each of them throughout their adolescent years. I didn't make my children feel safe and secure through my parenting approach.

Difficulty with Attachment: I thought my job as a parent was to provide a roof over their heads, put food on the table, protect them from harm, and guide them towards a life of independence. My understanding of what parenting looked like, derived from my foundation of freedom, did not include healthy attachments. I had no idea how to develop secure attachments with my children. This led me to show up in a repeated pattern as an emotionally distant parent, disengaged or emotionally unavailable.

Repeated Dysfunctional Patterns: My unresolved trauma led me to repeat the harmful patterns I experienced growing up. It also led me to introduce new harmful patterns such as physical and verbal abuse as well as emotional manipulation. I unknowingly perpetuated the cycle of dysfunction from my generation to the next, my children.

Low Self-Esteem and Shame: My low self-esteem and feelings of worthlessness also transferred on to my children. I had a hard time paying attention and listening to understand what my children wanted and needed from me. Ignoring their needs, while focusing on providing, or a relationship with a man, created the same feelings of being unseen with my children. I struggled for years with validating my children's unique and personal feelings, providing them with timely praise, or recognition that their interests and abilities may be vastly different than mine. One child shared with me how I made them feel growing up. I was recently told that they had a profane level of hatred and disdain for me. They would often refer to me to their inner circle, as that bitch. I felt invisible as a child and unfortunately made my children feel the same.

Overcompensation: I tried to overcompensate for material things I lacked in my upbringing. Incentivizing my children by buying them gifts or providing them with the latest and greatest gadgets, such as cell phones, tablets, or clothing. I even took my children on cruises and vacations to escape the monotony of our daily lives and to expose them to new cultures and experiences. This, however, was not an effective substitute for what was really missing, and that was healthy boundaries, communication, and emotional and psychological safety.

Increased Stress and Anxiety: I operated in constant fight or flight mode. My parenting style was fueled by feelings of loneliness, rejection, and anger. I was angry that I had to parent alone. I was angry that I didn't know what I was doing. The fear of failure or building a life like the one I had drove me to strive for further professional accomplishments, thinking that would make our lives better. My anger created a stressful and hostile environment for anyone around me, especially my children. They didn't know a mother filled with joy and happiness, they knew a distant and angry mother who worked all the time, failed to listen to their needs, and created an atmosphere where they walked on eggshells, afraid to speak up. They too, were trying to navigate this ph♥cked up world without a clue as to how to do so.

Difficulty in Modeling Healthy Relationships: I hadn't learned what healthy communication or effective conflict resolution looked like; therefore, I struggled to model these skills for my children. My memories included my mother nagging and criticizing my father, complaining about what he wasn't doing and explicitly telling him what he needed to do and how to do it. My father typically showed a response of silence and resolve, listening as she continued. Her nagging could have possibly been the reason for his nightly drinking, as a way of escaping from her. How could I model what I didn't know and hadn't seen?

Throughout the years, I tried to seek professional help, but the competing priorities of work, relationships, schooling, and parenting took precedence over my emotional and mental well-being. These examples illustrate how generational curses affected me as a young parent and how I passed some of the same conditioning onto my children.

According to the World Health Organization[2], a child who is abused is more likely to abuse others as an adult so that violence is passed down from one generation to the next. Sexual, physical, and emotional abuse are most likely witnessed and experienced before being repeated. The cycle of abuse, where an abused child grows up to become an abuser, is influenced by several psychological, emotional, and social factors. One reason is learned behavior – children who grow up in abusive environments often come to see such behavior as normal and may imitate it in our own relationships. Exposure to abuse can also lead to intergenerational trauma, where unresolved emotional pain from one generation affects future generations, creating patterns of dysfunctional behavior.

Children who experience abuse often lack healthy role models and may not know how to form relationships based on mutual respect and trust. The absence of positive examples can make it difficult for us to learn healthy conflict resolution skills. Abuse can also lead to low self-esteem and internalized shame, which can manifest in aggressive or abusive behaviors later in life to cope with unresolved pain. I had such difficulty with emotional regulation due to my childhood trauma that I struggled with managing my anger and emotions, for years.

I recognize that not all abused children become abusers. Many people will break the cycle of abuse through therapy, supportive relationships, and learning healthier coping strategies. I believe with the right support, it is possible to heal from past trauma and build a non-abusive, healthy future.

Not all generational curses will flow within the 4 walls of **your** home. There are also other generational curses to consider, including those within your family and close friends.

As young parents, we often rely on family members for childcare when needed. I found myself heavily relying upon family and friends to watch my children, without considering the type of care they would provide. While I knew their home was clean and didn't anticipate any harm to my children, I was unsure if potentially destructive behavior might be transferred.

Do you really need *that* family member to watch your children?

Have you stopped to consider whether they operate with the values and belief systems you want to instill in your children?

Take some time to consider the choices you make BEFORE you expose your children to other environments. This includes where you take your children for childcare, social settings, family activities, and even family members' homes.

My failure to ask myself those questions, before allowing others to care for my children, resulted in more painful and damaging experiences. It takes just one person to decide to make bold choices to change the trajectory for themselves and their family.

Memories Matter

My memories are fractured, riddled with painful feelings of rejection and not fitting in. I often tell people that I don't really remember my life experiences or have memories before the age of 10. I can look at pictures of events and activities and those often trigger some recollection, but not a full memory of what those experiences entailed.

Over the years, my children brought up memories that they can recall that I cannot remember. Their memories may be ones of joy and celebration like going to the zoo, road trips, amusement parks, and spending Christmas at my mother's house.

They also have memories that are bad. Like me working all the time, focusing on relationships with men, and not them. I never slowed down enough to listen and understand what they wanted and needed.

I now realize that with the hustle and bustle of life, the many distractions and competing priorities caused me to press through life, failing to fully capture the moments that mattered and translating those into lasting memories.

If you are anything like me where life has been tumultuous and you find yourself navigating one obstacle after another, you too may not realize the type of memories you are making with your child. I implore you to be *deliberate* and *intentional* when creating memories. If we want to stop generational curses, it starts with making changes in our own behavior.

- What are you doing to create positive and meaningful memories with your child? Take a moment to consider the following:

- Holiday and/or birthday traditions

- Vacations and time away from the day to day

- Cultural/Religious experiences/traditions

- Sports/Dance/Music - extracurricular activities

- Family gatherings/traditions

You may think your child is too young to remember a certain time in their lives, but I'm here to say that's not true. They **do** remember.

My children remember spending summers with their grandma due to my work responsibilities. With my mother, they remember camping and making s'mores. With my mother, they traveled to new states to learn about landmarks, museums, and history.

With me, my children remember my late nights working and me being unavailable for them to assist with homework or questions about life they may have had. With me, they remember the arguments and knock-down, drag-outs I had with significant others. They remember how angry I was and how afraid they were of coming to me for anything.

Memories Matter.

Now, don't get me wrong, my kids don't just remember the difficult and painful memories, they also remember the good times – the cruises, the birthday and graduation parties, the fact that I have been their #1 cheerleader and #1 fan for their entire lives. But in their most formidable years, the memories I created with them were unintentional and left traumatic scars.

As a parent, please remember it is all about building and creating a belief system in a brain that is forming and developing. What you do with your children matters.

What does it mean to raise a child?

Consider the belief system you want your child to have. If you want your child to have confidence – to feel safe and secure in who they are, and to feel loved and valued as part of a family – what specifically are you doing to instill this type of belief system?

Are you modeling confidence? Are you empowering your child to make decisions and learn from their experiences with optimism? Or are you modeling criticism and reprimanding your child for making mistakes?

Think about the last time you were disappointed in your child. What was the situation? How did you respond? Do you know how your child felt because of your response? Did you consider how your reaction would impact their feelings?

Are you establishing boundaries with and for your child? Are you sharing with them what you expect and clearly establishing the ground rules? Boundaries not only define rules and structure and consequences but also assist with preserving one's own mental health and well-being. Teaching the importance of boundaries is the foundation for self-respect and self-discipline.

Think about the last time your child didn't follow the rules or violated an established boundary. What were the consequences of their behavior? Are you consistent in following through with discipline or redirection when the child misbehaves?

Are you available for your child, intentionally planning uninterrupted time with just your child? As a single parent, I was busy with life while raising my children. Work, school, relationships, and parenting. Being physically present is *not* enough.

Think about a time when your child was hovering. You have been busy doing adult things, cooking, cleaning, working, watching television, trying to decompress, but they were in your presence, just waiting for you to engage with them. Did you recognize they wanted or needed attention? What was the situation? How did you respond?

Are you modeling loving behavior? Many parents have identified their own love language or even the love language of their partner, but do you know the love language of your child?

Think about how you show love for your child. Are you affectionate with hugs and kisses? Do you offer kind and encouraging words of affirmation?

Are you modeling intentional listening? Intentional listening is when you identify a specific purpose for attending to a conversation with an "intent to take action." You use all the usual active listening techniques (paying attention, summarizing, reflecting).

Do you allow your child's voice to be heard? Many parents who operate under the principle of children are to be seen and not heard. This should be far from the truth. Your child is unique and has a voice that may be very different from yours. Your child needs to be heard to feel valued.

Think about a time when your child was trying to get your attention. What was the situation? How did you respond? Did you stop to listen to what they had to say?

To have a confident child, you must model confidence and reinforce it is okay to make mistakes, and to learn from them with optimism.

- To make your child feel safe, set boundaries.

- To make your child feel secure, give them time, and pay attention to them.

Parents must also establish boundaries within the parent/child relationship. You are the parents – they are the child. Your child is not your friend, and they should not be exposed to adult conversations or problems. Find a different outlet if you need someone to talk to.

Consider the love language of your child. To make your child feel loved and valued, you must learn to display love in the way they need you to love them. This requires exploration and discovery. You must spend time with them – listen, learning, and understanding what makes them unique.

- What are you doing to deliberately develop their belief system?

- What do you want your child to believe in and about themselves and others?

- Are your actions generating the results you desire?

- How would you validate/confirm your impact on your children's development?

What is modeled, accepted, and reinforced in the home is what will be repeated and displayed through your child's relationships with others. So, if you created that safe and loving home referred to above, great! Your kids will emulate that by treating others with kindness and respect. If you didn't, you may receive some calls regarding your children's behavior.

I've included these questions because they are the things I didn't consider. The freedom in my foundation lacked structure and discipline with instilling a healthy belief system. My parents may have been intentional about providing us with freedom, but unfortunately the freedom in my foundation allowed me to create an environment for my children that lacked intentionality.

As a product of my environment, I was not deliberate and intentional as a parent. I didn't know what I was doing. I was a baby raising a baby without the proper context and framework to focus on developing her. I was too busy trying to survive and eager to learn.

The standards for relationship examples are built within the family unit and will trickle over into how your children build friendships and relationships. The baseline for what they see as good or bad is built upon the family experiences and translates into how your children choose their friends.

If 90% of brain development happens between birth and five years of age, be deliberate and intentional with the people you allow around your children.

As a teenage parent, wanting to parent differently than mine, I closely observed my friends to understand their family dynamics. I wanted to know if their family and home environment were one, I aspired to emulate. I knew I didn't want to raise Laisha, the same way I was raised.

I watched how they interacted with their parents. Did they show respect for their parents? If so, what did respect look like and why did they respect them? I listened to their stories about what it was like for them growing up and the consequences they suffered for bad behavior.

After dropping out of high school and earning my GED, at 17 years old I was living in my own 3-bedroom house, dating a 31-year-old married man and working for a local retailer. My friends became my most trusted advisors.

Branches & Limbs

The canopy or crown of a tree consists of branches, limbs, and leaves. Branches and limbs bring nutrients to the leaves as part of the canopy of the tree. While researching, I learned branches not only carry nutrients, but they also define how large the canopy or crown of the tree will be. According to Karli[3], a lifelong gardener, the branches of the tree will also store energy through dormant periods and times of non-ideal conditions, providing sustenance from which the tree can survive.

Our relationships with close friends or extended family are like branches, where the relationships can weather the changing of the seasons and the roughness of storms right along with you.

These relationships may last years and even decades. You could possibly even lose touch with them but can always reach out and pick up right where you left off. These people are your branches. Our friends assist us when weathering the storms of life and providing us with the food (wisdom, guidance, and support) we need to survive. My friends were my only branches; I needed them to survive.

Friends, Mentors, & Coaches

When we were young, everyone was our **friend**. We made friends on the first day of school, and they remained our friends until they hurt our feelings. As we got older, we started forming friendships that lasted longer than just a few weeks.

We may have friends from elementary to high school, college, and previous work environments. Some of these friendships will last decades or a lifetime. Do you have to talk every day? No. Do you have to talk every month or year? No. But when you do connect, it is like you haven't missed a beat!

However, some friendships fizzle away as time continues to lapse. Our interests change, our priorities change, and our friendships change, and that is okay. Some people are *not* meant to go the distance with you!

I have learned that friends play an important role in how we grow and develop our personalities, standards, and belief systems. Our friends help us process the good, the bad, and the ugly times we experience in life.

When we get exciting news, we get this emotional rush, a desire to share this information with people who matter. This is the time when we call our biggest supporter, a parent, a sibling, or best friend. We want to align with others in our journey of good news. Our friends may not always share the same enthusiasm or excitement. You may expect it, but don't receive it.

A great thing about friends is the differences and uniqueness we bring to the relationship. Not all friendships are built on commonality and similarities; some are built on differences. It is my belief that differences in relationships help us learn and grow, if we allow ourselves to see things from an alternative perspective.

When non-ideal conditions exist, when we are going through a tough time in life, a breakup, loss of a loved one, a job loss, we often reach out to friends for advice and comfort. We need someone's fresh perspective to help us assess how we look at things. As you grow in life, you will realize that some of your friends do not have the wisdom and/or experience to help you navigate through a particular obstacle. Find a therapist. Find new friends.

For example, when I was married and going through challenges, I often reached out to certain married friends for advice. What do you do when your spouse does x, y, or z? Was I wrong for responding in the way that I did? What could make our relationship get back on track? After years of seeking advice from others on how to navigate marital challenges, I started to realize some things. Our friends will often "side" with us and fail to offer the objectivity of a therapist, sponsor, or mentor.

Advice is based on **opinion**.

Wisdom is based on **experience**.

How in the world would my marriage get better if I was seeking advice from a friend who was just as inexperienced, confused, or unhappy as me? How would my marriage benefit from getting advice from a friend who was cheating on their spouse? It wouldn't. While I am a fiercely loyal person, I have learned that I must be *selective* when it comes to who I connect with on certain matters. Be careful who you listen to because all your friends do not have experience in the areas where you may need help. These people may only be able to offer advice. It is important to seek friendships or mentors to help you navigate through life by offering you insights based upon experience and wisdom.

Advice is suggestions or recommendations based on someone's **opinion**.

Wisdom is suggestions or recommendations based on someone's **experience**.

A pastor once said, when you buy someone's opinion, you are buying their lifestyle. I could not seek advice from just anyone. If I wanted wisdom, I needed advice from people who were a living example of what I wanted my relationship to look like.

Friends come from different backgrounds and have a variety of life experiences. While friends may offer advice, not all friends will provide you with wisdom. Just like branches on trees, some friendships are solid and strong - designed to stick with you and weather the storm – while others are weak and brittle - the ones that instantly snap when a little pressure is applied.

Have you ever met someone and felt instantly connected? Whether it existed as a commonality in your career or spiritual interests, travel destinations, or fraternity or sorority affiliation. In many interactions with others, you will notice that most people love talking about themselves. This leads me to believe that most people are willing to help others, by talking about themselves to pour into others from their own experiences. My purpose is to pour into the development of others, and I have mentored people for more than 30 years.

Mentors are not friends, but they may feel like friends at times. Mentors are individuals you trust and rely upon for their wisdom and expertise. These are often people who have lived different experiences and are an example of something you admire and respect. Mentors exist in community, political, and social settings such as churches, civic organizations or political offices, fraternities and sororities, and professional and educational settings such as work or school. Mentors may be found anywhere.

A mentoring relationship is often informal, long-term, and has a broad focus. When considering whether to seek a mentor, you must first identify your goals. Be specific and deliberate with what you would like to accomplish from the relationship. Mentors volunteer their time to work with you, and please consider that everyone's number one asset is time.

Once you know what you need, look within your current network. Does anyone you know have the skills or experience you are seeking? Consider joining professional organizations or attending networking events. Volunteering in the community is also another great way to get out and meet new people.

Whenever you connect with someone who is willing to invest in you, be sure to be on time for meetings, be respectful, and demonstrate appreciation. In my mentoring relationships, I always explain to my mentees that I will show up and give them as much or as little as they require from me. It is up to me to establish appropriate boundaries and up to them to get the most from our relationship. I expect them to extract from me as much or as little as they want. Life is hard and if I can help, I will.

Think of someone you respect or admire. What do you want to learn from them? How can this person help you become the best version of yourself? It may feel scary at first, the thought of asking someone for help. However, it will not hurt you and will only help you if they say yes.

If you lose your job, you can find another one. If you break up with your significant other, you can find a new relationship. If you lose money on a poor investment or business decision, you can earn more money. Money isn't your greatest asset, time is. Time is the one thing that we will never get back.

Your #1 Asset is TIME.

In the complexity of today's world, juggling the balance between work, life, and family, many professionals are turning to **Coaches** who are compensated for their wisdom and expertise. Coaching relationships are often formal, short-term, and narrowly focused. There are life coaches, executive coaches, business coaches, and even recovery coaches to assist individuals navigating the dynamics of loved ones with addiction and mental health struggles.

The benefits of working with a coach are personalized guidance, improved decision-making ability, accountability, motivation, and improved confidence. Coaching is about helping an individual realize and achieve their greatest potential.

Intimate Partners

I am a firm believer that every person in this world wants to be loved in a way that only an intimate partner can love. We want to feel both the butterflies in the pit of our stomach and the comfort of knowing there is someone there for us and to have our back. A partner to be there with us step by step and day by day experiencing the challenges of this ph♥cked up and often complicated and difficult life. We need a partner and friend, a companion and lover, a cheerleader and that safe space to go to when things get tough.

Sometimes we create expectations for what this intimate partner should look like based upon the foundation our parents, family, and friends established for us. We either decide to emulate what we saw or go to the extreme and seek a polarized opposite! Did you date or marry someone just like your dad or your mom? We tend to gravitate towards characteristics that are familiar and recognizable, whether they are good or bad. According to a recent research project at Michigan State University, people tend to show a love interest in people who mirror characteristics of their parents[4].

Sometimes, if we are lucky, we find a great balance between the two, someone who reminds us of all the good things from home yet is different enough to challenge us to grow beyond what has been familiar. However we choose, it is often a byproduct of our own environment and belief systems that operate as our guide in selecting an intimate partner.

Remember, the brain doesn't fully develop until at least 25 and I was far from that. My brain wasn't fully developed, but my attitude was! With the freedom and flexibility to do what I wanted, when I wanted, I felt empowered to make adult decisions. As distorted as my perspective was, and being just a child, I sought comfort and validation from my intimate relationships. I jumped into relationships on both feet, **all in**!

I will spare you all the details of the stupid things I did as a teenager and young adult. I will also spare you all the details of the tumultuous failing in and out of love cycle I have embraced for nearly my entire life. But the whole intention of this book is to share some lessons learned.

These sentiments apply whether you are a teenager or an adult.

Do your homework before you give your body away to another.

- Do your homework before you give your body away to another.
  - ° Wrap it up!
  - ° If you choose to raw dog it and have unprotected sex, please remember there are consequences that you may not be prepared for.
    - ▪ Are you ready to be a parent 9-10 months from

now?

  - Are you ready to no longer live for yourself, but for the nurturing and wellbeing of another for the next 20 years? If not, take the necessary actions to mitigate the risk of pregnancy.

- What do you know about your partner's family history?

  ○ What is your partner's belief system?

  ○ What are your partner's family dynamics?

    - How much do you really know about who gave birth to your partner?

    - Is there a history of mental illness?

    - Is there a history of drug abuse?

    - Is there a history of family violence?

- Sex isn't just a physical act, it is spiritual, intimate, and it creates a soul tie. Be *intentional* with whom you engage in intimate relationships and sexual activity.

Now, let me tell you why these things are so important.

I got pregnant at 15 and delivered a baby girl at 16. Is that a surprise? Laisha's dad and I were both involved in gangs, and he was subsequently arrested when Laisha was just six weeks old. He spent the first five years of her life in prison. When he got out, he built a new life, with a new family, as we were busy building ours. Do you think his new life involved his first child? No.

Consequences of my choices:

- I was a single, teenaged parent.

- As a parent, I was absent from my children's full life. While I may have been physically present, I was not deliberate and intentional with the choices I made as I was still trying to figure out how to navigate life. I was never fully attuned to what Laisha needed.

- My mother was more involved in raising my children than she should have been. While my mother's intentions appeared to be pure, the consequences of her influence left scars in the relationship between my children and me.

- Generational curses were repeated (my own, now onto my children):

  ○ Low self-esteem

  ○ Feelings of rejection

  ○ Lack of self-worth

It seems easy to highlight the negative consequences of my choices, as they were so monumental for not only my first child but also me. However, there are quite a few positive things that came from my choice to give birth to Laisha and to raise her as best as I could.

I have a beautiful, talented, and gifted 34-year-old daughter. She holds three college degrees: a bachelor, master's, and juris doctorate. She is pouring her energy into others as a state-licensed attorney, representing and defending those who are often overlooked by society. A young woman who took a very different path in life from mine, yet very similar to my passion of pouring into the lives of others. ❤️

At 21, I found myself pregnant again. This time, I was in a toxic relationship with a boyfriend who was recently released from prison, who was out having sex with another woman, while I was in the hospital in labor. Looks like I didn't learn a thing from having sex and creating the first child. Truth is, I didn't. I was so young and immature, looking for self-esteem, validation, and companionship in all the wrong places.

When I mentioned taking the time to get to know you or an intimate partner, let me tell you **AGAIN**, why this is so important.

- Drug use and abuse have impacted my family.

- Prison has impacted my family.

- Mental illness has impacted my family.

These are just a few things that plagued my intimate partner's family and now are replicated in my family. Now, don't get me wrong, I have similar negative influences that come from my side of the family due to my family's generational curses. So, it is important to consider both family histories and choose wisely.

Intimate partners should enhance your life and create a space of safety, security, and comfort.

You must decide if you are willing to create a deliberate and intentional plan to break these curses in how you raise your children. It can happen, but you must be intentional with your choices.

Intimate partners should enhance your life by creating a space of safety, security, comfort, and supporting you as you realize the best version of yourself. They should help bring out the best in you.   They hold you accountable for making decisions that support growth and personal development.   If your person is not your friend and companion, someone to share your innermost feelings with, your lover, your partner, your cheerleader, your safe space when life gets tough, then Ph❤ckIt! Run!

Leaves

As part of the canopy, leaves provide shade and even habitats or homes for other plants and animals. Leaves produce the primary food source for the tree by converting sunlight into energy. As the seasons change, the leaves of deciduous trees will change colors and eventually fall from the tree.

Just as leaves are essential for a tree's survival, friends play a vital role in our emotional and social well-being. They bring positivity, joy, and support, helping us "thrive" in life and providing us with the energy and encouragement we need to face challenges.

Leaves come and go with the seasons changing. Some friends stick around for a lifetime, but just like the leaves, some relationships die and wither away. Despite seasons changing, each leaf – like each friend – ads something unique to our lives. Just as leaves help protect the tree and provide shade, friends offer comfort and protection helping us feel understood and cared for.

Friends & Acquaintances

Friendships may fade away over time, and those friends turn into acquaintances. Remember I mentioned that you will sometimes reach out to a friend, looking for advice, and that person doesn't respond in the way in which you were expecting. Rather than offering you support or positive energy, they offer negative energy and vibes.

You have the right to change your mind on how you classify a relationship. Just because someone was your friend, when you learn more about who they are and what they represent, you have the right to change your mind. You may have heard the adage from Maya Angelou, "When someone shows you who they are, believe them." Friendships must be evaluated from time to time, especially when negative energy surfaces. This may be the time to move that person from friend to acquaintance.

You have the right to change your mind!

The canopy of your tree is your *inner circle*. You decide who is in your inner circle.   Your canopy is made up of friends and acquaintances, who nourish your growth and development. When those leaves die and fall, it symbolizes the relationships you need to let go of. Just as a tree sheds unproductive leaves to thrive, you, too, must release unhelpful connections to make space for new, enriching ones. You decide who is part of your canopy covering you.

Choices We Make to Attach to or Detach from Relationships

In the words of Bishop T. D. Jakes, "You can't choose your devil, but you can choose your reaction." While we cannot choose our parents, or the family dynamics in which we are raised, we do have the ability to make more informed decisions when deciding who should remain in our lives. Consider making the choice to dive into your family history to understand and discover what belief systems were instilled in you.

- Did your parents or family instill a belief system that you want to reinforce within your own family?

- Are there generational curses or relationship dynamics that you aren't aware of?

- What are your memories from your childhood?

- What types of family traditions were instilled in you?

You may be like me, where you don't remember your parents instilling any deliberate and intentional family traditions, such as holiday traditions. This doesn't mean they didn't exist; it could be that the drama and trauma you experienced outweighed anything positive, and it is hard to remember. Despite negative things that may have happened to you along the way, you are responsible for charting your own course. Either way, consider your family history and make an intentional decision about how you choose to live your life moving forward.

Friends, mentors, and intimate partners come and go, and some will be there for a lifetime. Make informed decisions about the people you choose to engage with, it's about being intentional about the people, not just the decision. Remember, you have influence over how your children choose people as well. It is okay for you or your child to choose to define relationships differently, at any point in time in the relationship. Our decisions should help accelerate our purpose on this earth. We are the authors of our stories.

It is important to protect your roots, and there may be times to pluck up that which was planted. There may be times when a branch breaks off or you need to prune it away yourself. Don't be afraid to lose some leaves, they weren't designed to stay with the tree forever.

Lessons Learned

- Family - We cannot change who our family members are, nor can we change the belief system that was established for us early on in life, but we can choose to redefine our own belief system based upon our own life experiences and desires to break generational curses.

- Memories matter – What lasting impressions have you made? What positive memories will you make?

- Relationships may change over time, and that's okay. You have the right to change your mind.

- Advice is different from wisdom. Find mentors and coaches to choose wisdom.

- Choose your intimate partners wisely. The consequences of choosing a partner not equally yoked can have a generational impact.

- Remember, Sex Works!

Ph❤ckIt! I'm a Maverick

I didn't know the meaning of **a maverick** until I looked up the definition in 2022. My only frame of reference to a maverick was the university mascot where my mother taught for more than 40 years. After researching the meaning and reflecting upon my experiences, I would soon discover that a maverick means much more to me than a mascot.

According to **Merriam-Webster**[5], the definition of a *maverick* is:

1. an unbranded range animal *especially*: a motherless calf

2. an independent individual who doesn't go along with a group or party

According to **Dictionary.com**[6], the definition of a *maverick* is:

1. an unbranded calf, cow, or steer, especially an unbranded calf that is separated from its mother.

2. a lone dissenter, as an intellectual, an artist, or a politician, who takes an independent stand apart from his or her associates.

3. a person pursuing rebellious, even potentially disruptive policies or ideas.

According to **Vocabulary.com**[7], the definition of a *maverick* is:

1. noun - someone who exhibits great independence in thought and action.

2. noun - an unbranded range animal (especially a stray calf); belongs to the first person who puts a brand on it.

3. adjective - independent in behavior or thought.

A Maverick. A motherless calf – an unbranded range animal. I had no idea that a maverick was considered motherless. I knew it was an animal and that a maverick was often revered as someone who did their own thing, but motherless? As an adoptee, I have often felt motherless and can relate so much to the definitions described above. Unbranded, or unclaimed, motherless, rebellious, and independent in both thought and action, accurately describes the woman I embrace, love, and have become.

I didn't know I was a maverick until March 2022 when I was approached through a professional networking site about an amazing career opportunity. I was shocked when a search firm for my favorite NBA team was contacting me to be their next Chief Human Resources Officer. I hadn't thought of leaving my current job as Chief Administrative Officer, since I was promoted after just a few months with the organization. How in the world could I turn down exploring an exciting opportunity with my favorite sports team of all time? I couldn't, so I engaged in the exploration process.

After an initial screening by the recruiter, I advanced to the next stage of interviewing with the hiring manager. She was an extraordinary woman with a trailblazing path of service to the communities she served. After a fruitful and engaging conversation, I advanced to the next stage.

I had to complete the Predictive Index (PI), a behavioral assessment that measures behavioral drives and cognitive ability. After taking the PI assessment, I was sent a link with an overview of my results. I read the report and saw the definition of maverick, which read: "A maverick is an innovative, *outside the box* thinker, who is undaunted by failure." I said, "Yep, that accurately describes me."

I continued the interviewing process by participating in a recorded video interview and a panel interview with multiple executives. Finally, I completed the job application which included providing references. I just knew that God was looking down on me, telling me, "Get ready, daughter, it is your time to shine." I was so excited and prepared to take the leap of faith into a new city and a new, exciting career.

And just like that, the organization ghosted me! In case you are not familiar with the term, *ghosting* means they ended conversations with me without any explanation and withdrew from all communication. In my case, I eventually got a follow-up call a few months later. They decided to go in a different direction, leveraging a different type of skillset than what I had to offer.

> # You shouldn't want anything that wasn't intentionally designed just for you.

Professionally, I had more lateral movement than upward movement, so to have an NBA team look at me, and to get as far as I did in the interview process, was a comforting reassurance that I still had "it." The courtship from the team and the expanded network of connections gave me reassurance in my skills, abilities, and capacity to do more.

I was like, "Okay God, I don't want anything that you haven't intentionally designed for me." So, I tucked my hurt feelings away and focused on my current employer and my responsibilities to be the best leader I could be.

Just Because You Can, Doesn't Mean You Should

2018 was one of the toughest years of my life. My mother suffered a life-altering stroke, I went through a divorce, and my son Jamal was arrested and sentenced to prison for 7 years. Jamal's arrest was precipitated by years of substance abuse and untreated trauma.

I wanted to, I *needed* to, help save others from the effects of mental illness and addiction. With a vision to eliminate the mental health stigma in the Black community, I launched DM Phoenix. A state licensed residential treatment center for individuals with co-occurring conditions.

While I was able to serve a dozen or so men, a fatal flaw in the business plan caused my business to operate in the non-profit space rather than as a for-profit venture. After investing more than $200,000 in that business, I made the decision to take the lessons learned, close the doors, pick up the pieces, and move on.

Now, trust me, that was not an easy decision to make. I invested almost all my 401K savings, invested dollars from others, and countless hours investing in the formation and launching of this business. As someone who has been fortunate to always rebound through the grace and mercy of God, I felt as if I was bailing too soon on such a noble mission and purpose that was serving the community.

I thought to myself, *God, you gave me this brain and this heart to serve others!* God's chastening pierced me to my soul and at the same time freed me to forgive myself for the decisions I made. Once again, I was in the space of picking up the pieces and moving forward with life. I closed my business, sold my house, and moved to another state. God had to yell at me, because I often don't listen, "Just because you can, doesn't mean you should!"

I had another epiphany. There were so many lessons in God's clear declaration to me that day. As someone who believes I can take on just about any obstacle, it is humbling to stop and reflect upon the statement. *Just because you can, doesn't mean you should*, resonated in my soul.

- Just because you can help that person, doesn't mean you should.

- Just because you have the knowledge and insight to make something happen, doesn't mean it is your burden to bear.

- Just because you can say that doesn't mean you should.

> # Just because you can, doesn't mean you should.

My mouth has gotten me into so many situations that at one point in my career, I had to learn another valuable lesson which is to edit myself. Many of us struggle with the ability to control ourselves when we feel like we must get our point across. In many 12-step programs, they teach the importance to understand what is in our control and what is not. The ability to edit yourself is in your control.

Chutes & Ladders™ *Navigating My Career*

Do you remember the game *Chutes & Ladders?*™ The game is designed to challenge players to get to the top of the game board using ladders, without landing on one of the chutes, forcing the player back down the game board. The player who reaches the top first wins the game.

After more than 30 years in the workplace, I found myself reflecting on what my professional journey has been like over the years. This game, in my opinion, says it all. It is all about trying to climb the ladder to the top: the top of a corporation, a department, an organization, a team, the top of a pay range, consistently seeking the next level.

Most people are searching for something more. While not everyone is destined for leadership roles, most people still strive to earn as much money as possible to provide for themselves and their families, seeking prestige and titles of importance along the way. Many adults are climbing the corporate ladder. Some climb the ladder for a short period of time and "make it" to the top, while others climb for a lifetime.

There are contributing factors that accelerate the climb such as education, experience, and let's face it, personality, appearance, and our personal network. These factors can make a huge difference in how quickly you climb those ladders.

I recently learned from my adoptive mother that one of the reasons she adopted me was to provide me with "White privilege." Yes, you read that correctly. White privilege. The simple fact that she thought she could provide me, a Black woman, with White privilege, is indicative of what White privilege is all about - the position of being superior or having societal privilege to another race, based purely on the color of one's skin. She thought that by adopting me, a biracial child, that she, a White woman, could influence my life's trajectory, by instilling White privilege in me.

One cannot give a person who is Black, Brown, or any other color, something that is reserved for White people. When I challenged her intentions, she referenced my academic endeavors and how well I performed academically in college. Again, disgusted with her statement of intentions, I reiterated that her intentions would never materialize, because no matter how she viewed me, the world would always view me as a Black woman.

A deliberate thing I know my parents instilled in me was the importance of education. Both parents had master's degrees and worked in higher education. Despite having a tumultuous start to my academic endeavors, I, too, earned my master's degree to accelerate my career to the next level.

As a Black woman, I felt the need to achieve every academic expectation, every certification, and to participate in every training opportunity for development, to remain competitive and relevant for career growth and momentum. Let's face it. It seems clear that more is expected from people of color in order for us to j claim that proverbial seat at the table!

A Black Maverick & Goliath

You may remember the story of David and Goliath from the Bible. David was a small shepherd boy, and Goliath was a giant he had to face in a battle. My Goliath was a giant global corporation I found myself married to for eleven years. For a moment, well, a long moment, I thought I was on the right path, the one where upward career momentum was happening.

I was a director at Goliath, making six figures and frequently traveling on corporate jets. I had a corporate credit card, a team of 11 direct reports, and access to any and every development opportunity, or so I thought. At the age of 34, I found myself in a space of gratitude, proud of my accomplishments, until I crashed into a glass ceiling, headfirst.

I knew my team and I were producing amazing results, and I assumed that my leadership and our team's performance would speak for itself. When my leader vacated his position, I didn't even think about applying for his role. I assumed my brand and team reputation would create another inroad for promotion and growth within Goliath. You know what they say about the word *assume*...I was about to make an absolute ass of myself.

I was navigating multiple obstacles in my personal life and attempting to maintain a level of sanity. I don't even know if the position was posted, but I was shocked when our new leader was announced. A woman with limited internal experience and not a lot of overall experience in the field was my new leader. My mind began to instantaneously wonder, why wasn't I considered for the promotional opportunity? Did she get the job because she was tall, attractive, younger than me, and White? With all the chaos going on with me personally, I didn't say anything about feeling passed over, but I definitely felt some kind of way on the inside.

After nearly a year of working with her, she was promoted again, this time to an officer of the company. My team and I continuously made significant contributions that catapulted her success. My team and I created and implemented cutting-edge programs, projects, and change management initiatives at the national level. Each program and project we worked on encompassed a great deal of complexity. Yet, with little to no contributions to the actual work that had been done, she was being promoted, and I didn't understand.

Therefore, during my performance evaluation, I felt it was appropriate to express my concerns and provide her with feedback. Isn't that the right time to offer your leader feedback?

While she was focused on providing me with feedback on my performance, my mouth decided to have some courage (*my mouth was watering, waiting to pounce*). I wasn't even processing the fact that my overall performance review was good, I was anticipating the moment for me to speak. When she got to a point where the feedback became constructive, I couldn't hear anything constructive and/or negative, I just wanted to say what I wanted to say.

Remember, just because you can, doesn't mean you should!

I was going to let her know just how frustrated I was and said, "The only reason you were promoted, was because of the work my team and I have done!" She just looked at me, with an incredulous look and said something to the effect that I should not talk to her in that manner; that it seemed to be disrespectful.

Disrespectful? I didn't think I was being disrespectful; I felt like I was being honest and speaking my truth. All I was doing was advocating for myself. However, there was a dynamic in place that I was oblivious to at that point in my life. While I knew I was a Black woman climbing the corporate ladder, I lacked the full comprehension of what that entailed. How dare I, a Black woman, challenge the opinion of my White leader is how I took her response. That is exactly how I felt she was looking at me during my performance review. While she didn't say it, her subsequent actions, said it all.

Let's just say that my mouth, capable of saying whatever I allowed it to say, gave me a costly lesson. A week or so later, I was written up or disciplined for being disrespectful. I tried to speak to her leader, to get the disciplinary action overturned, and that didn't work well for me either. The executive said, "This is one of those tough lessons you are going to have to learn from."

> # Does everything you want to say need to be said to an actual audience?
>
> # No!

I had a level of respect for our executive leader, as she was a person of color, very poised, polished, and FIERCE! On the surface, it appeared that she navigated a male-dominated environment, paid her dues, and was sitting in a top position at

Goliath. She carried herself with confidence and I admired this about her, so I took the lesson learned. The lesson? There are consequences for speaking your mind, and just because I wanted to say something didn't mean that I should.

I allowed my emotions to get the best of me. I allowed my amygdala to get hijacked. Don't allow this to happen to you. Learn from my experiences. At this point in my career, I learned to edit myself. Ask yourself the following questions:

- Does everything you want to say have to be said to an actual audience? No.

- Write it down. Getting things off your brain onto paper is often as therapeutic as saying something to someone. Just get it out of your head and off your mind.

- Is this the mountain you want to die on? Is what you have to say necessary? No.

- Who else can you talk to, to allow you to sort out your emotions and help you determine if a response is even required?

When you are frustrated with the behaviors and actions of others, be cautious when venting up to superiors, be confident venting outside of your work environment, and never vent down to people who report to you.

Learn to edit yourself!

The executive referenced above had respect for my direct leader. I am not sure it extended beyond the fact that she hired her and promoted her, but there was a clear alignment and support for her. After the disciplinary action was administered, I felt it was necessary for me to move on to something new. I didn't want to stay in an environment where I was not going to be recognized for my performance and the performance of my team. So, I opted for a career pivot.

As I applied for various internal roles, exploring opportunities for growth and exposure to new parts of Goliath, rather than allowing my skills and abilities speak for themselves in the interviewing process, my leader tried to thwart one specific opportunity to leave her team. This White woman, my leader, felt it was necessary to tell the hiring team that I was disrespectful towards her, and they shouldn't consider my candidacy for the operations role. What she didn't know was that there was like mindedness waiting for me on the other side of that promotion. I got the job. My new executive team consisted of leadership team members who were Black, just like me. They recognized my former leader's attempted interference, knew what I was capable of, and hired me into a role that was a higher level than the one I would be leaving.

This was a major career pivot and career-defining opportunity for me to showcase my talents. Transitioning from a corporate support function of human resources to operations is not an easy task, nor does it happen very often. Operations is where revenue is generated for a company, and operational leaders at Goliath are positioned to make lots of money if they perform well.

My first year, I was recognized as Leader of the Year within my region. Over the next several years, I was so proud to see the growth and development within my team. Team members were getting promoted, and our team's performance was generating strong financial results. I was finally climbing a new financial ladder. I made more money than my parents. I was able to take my children on international vacations, and I was under 40. The Black girl magic was happening, and I was doing my thing, until someone said I wasn't.

Ten years into my career, I encountered a force, a new leader, who had very little interest in my success and growth at this company. I was one of a handful of Black leaders in my position across the country. I was the only Black person in my role west of the Mississippi River Delta. In a company of our size, one would think there would be hundreds of Black executives or leaders, but that was not the case. In a company that employed millions, there were probably less than 50 Black executives. Yep, that's it, a few dozen.

As I was feeling this negative energy from my new leader, I started noticing all the Black executives and corporate leaders sliding down the chutes and out the door. First, it was a chief level executive, then it was a few vice presidents. The list kept growing.

Remember, I was the only Black person in my respective position in the western half of the US. And let me tell you, my performance was being meticulously measured by a constantly moving target. My leader was so hyper focused on what was happening in my area of the business, he chose to visit me and my territory while I was on vacation! Who does that? He was clear on his opinion of me, my skills, and my abilities. He thought I should have stayed in a support role of HR vs. operations, and he ridiculed me for making the career pivot five years prior. He made snide comments like, "This isn't corporate and pretty. This is operations." He was a complete jerk.

There was a story that circulated during my tenure with that company. While I cannot find the actual document, I am going to summarize it to the best of my recollection. There was a metaphor comparing boots and shoes to employees at Goliath.

The boots were the ones who were the bedrock and foundation of the company. The shoes were the people who were merely a means to an end of getting stuff done. The shoes weren't designed to be long term employees, just ones to get in, add temporary value, and get out.

Now, if you were part of the boot legacy, you were a lifer. You could count on career growth beyond your own thought of trajectory. Residual and perpetual income, exceptions would be made for the boots, regardless of poor judgment or inferior performance; if you were part of the boot crew, you were golden, and nothing would damage your future with the company – yes, up to and including creating and perpetuating false narratives to cover up for one another.

Remember that executive I mentioned who was so sharp and fierce? Well, I later learned that she was part of the boots crew. She was related to a member of the Board of Directors. The roots of the boot crew ran deep.

Whether I wanted to leave or not, the writing was on the wall, and it was time for me to go. The chute was opening and rather than allowing a new negative force to design an exit plan for me, I designed my own. For the next twelve months, I watched **every** Black leader I knew sign a severance package, slide down the chute, and exit the company. I chose an alternative path. I leveraged the benefits and resources available to me, and I made sure I left the company on my own terms, free from the restraints of a severance agreement, and free to speak my truth.

There were a few of us Black leaders who would connect to discuss the significant transition happening, with all of us questioning the reasons behind the massive movement down the chutes. No matter how far up one Black leader had climbed, they were all going down the Goliath chute. It became apparent, Black leaders were being exited from the company, and fast!

One may think that I learned a lesson about how corporate America works, while sitting there literally watching people's lives transform, but I didn't quite get it yet. As I reflect on the boots and shoe story, it appeared to be all about privilege, access, and placement. Sound familiar? This was what my mother was trying to provide for me, yet no matter how hard she tried, I still ended up going down a career chute because I am Black.

For Black professionals in corporate America, there are far more times when we have "oh shit" moments that lead to sliding down the chute. I am sure you know of plenty of "oh shit" moments in your career.

- Did that just happen?
- Did he/she just say that to me?
- Are you serious right now?

As Black men and women navigate this ph♥cked up professional environment, trying to define our career growth paths, we find ourselves asking questions of ourselves, our friends and mentors, trying to understand the situation, determining what actions to take next.

Ph❤ck This Job!

I recently read *White Fragility*[8], a beautifully written book by antiracist educator, Robin DiAngelo. While there is so much to unpack from her teachings and my learnings, one thing that stood out to me was the system was not designed for Black people to grow and thrive. When I say the system, I am referring to systems of power, control, influence, and money.

Oh, how I wish I had this book 20 years ago! Although it was just published in 2018, the insight she provides, from a White woman's perspective, is profound. Every person in leadership should read this book, especially, White people, because she wrote the book for that demographic. She says, "Start by reflecting on your own experience of being a White person.[9]" The intention is for White people to explore their defensiveness and responses when their behaviors and assumptions about race are questioned.

The moment I took a deep dive into the book, I wanted to order the book for my previous leader at FTM, a fictitious name I created for this former employer. She is the epitome of White privilege, and her fragility created discord in my soul. These are my lessons learned.

Do you remember the *Animaniacs* cartoon character, Katie Ka-Boom?

According to *Animaniacs* Fandom[10], *"Katie Ka-Boom is an innocent 16-year-old girl who greatly overreacts to trivially upsetting situations and literally turns into a flaming monster before subsequently exploding, usually leaving the family home in ruins. Katie is very overreactive, ill-tempered, and emotionally difficult. When she's in her normal self, she is actually a lovely, innocent, and nice girl. Though when she goes "Ka-Boom" (hence her last name), she turns into any destructive monster, literally."*

Katie Ka-Boom describes a previous CEO I worked with perfectly. On the surface, she was kind and caring, and I immediately connected with her. I brought my best self to the team, prepared to support the organization's mission. Because of how I was raised, as well as my own traumatic experiences, I trust people up front. I view the world in terms of rainbows and unicorns. I inherently believe people are good. And this was my first mistake with Katie Ka-Boom.

My nature is to bring myself authentically to all engagements, regardless of my audience.

As a professional, with nearly 30 years of leading people, my passion has always been to invest in the development of others. This is evident in my career path in human resources. As a strategic partner, with both an operations and people lens, I bring my experience to assist and guide in business strategy, change management, and human resource initiatives.

Therefore, coming into this senior leadership role, I brought my whole Black maverick self to the team. At first, Katie welcomed me enthusiastically. My fresh perspective and approach were celebrated, until it wasn't.

Am I The Bridge?

I had a seat at the table. The C-Suite table. I felt as if I had arrived. But, arrived where?

As I sat at the board room table, listening to board members ask questions of a candidate during an interview for the vacant chief financial officer (CFO) position, I watched the candidate's body language as question after question appeared to make him extremely uncomfortable. The board members, who were asking questions, had worked with him not only as a fellow board member, but one was also his previous leader at another company.

His eyes glimpsed in my direction, and I could see his shock and confusion as to why they were asking such pointed questions, clearly designed to force an uncomfortable response. This candidate, unlike the other two, was Black. The emotions of disbelief and rage began to build within my heart. I knew they were asking questions of him that were not asked of other candidates. Why were they treating him like that? He is a fellow board member and clearly qualified to take the role.

As the interview concluded, I quickly left the board room and headed to my office. I ran into the candidate in the break room. I looked at him, with tears in my eyes, and said, "I am so sorry you just went through that."

I don't really remember what he said in response, but I remember it was comforting and something along the lines of, "You didn't do anything wrong. Thank you for being there for me."

I had to get out of there! I rushed to my office, closed my door, and wept. After a few moments, I left the office to find a way to reset. I had to continue working for the rest of the day. It was hard. I felt like God was using me as a bridge between what has always been and what it should be. It stood as a painful place to be. It stretched me beyond my comfort zone. It tortured me to see and feel the agony of every Black and Brown person who has experienced this pain of racism and discriminatory practices. That week, I thought, *"Okay God, I am the **bridge**."* I prayed that my efforts and actions would provoke a change at FTM.

It was a scene all too familiar, unfolding in that boardroom, and we, the only two Black leaders present, were the sole witnesses to its true nature. The frustration of our unique perspective was palpable. The other executives, seemingly obliviously, unwittingly altered the entire atmosphere with their questions and demeanor. What was intended to be a straightforward review of qualifications morphed into a degrading and belittling experience for a fellow professional, a highly qualified Black man.

The new CFO was hired, and it was not the equally qualified Black man. No, it was Mighty Mouse, a short little White woman. You know, the little mouse who frequently belts out, "Here I come to save the day!" Katie Ka-Boom was now joined at the hip by Mighty Mouse, another White woman. Have you heard when two or more are gathered….and I am not talking about the biblical gathering either. I was now encamped in a whirlwind of magnified White privilege, fragility, entitlement, and chaos.

Our organization served an underrepresented community that consisted of Black and Brown people of color in a low socioeconomic community. I felt an intrinsic pressure to make things better. I was the only person of color in leadership. A fundamental responsibility of my role was mitigating risk and identifying solutions.

With my background in operations and an early stint in my career in operational audits, I tend to see things through the lens of exceptions. I often say, *I can't unlearn what I already know.* When I uncovered irregularities in company practices, ones that have significant consequences because of federal regulations, I shared my concerns with Katie. When my concerns went unacknowledged and unaddressed, I went to the Board.

After I spoke to the Board, standing on my principles of integrity and moral values, the energy from Katie shifted from enthusiasm and celebration to suspicion of ulterior motives. My character and actions came into question, subsequently leading to me being stripped of certain responsibilities. Mighty Mouse conspired with Katie to create and perpetuate false narratives. It appeared to be clear that Mighty Mouse felt there was far too much power in a Black woman's control, and she manipulated Katie's previously appreciated value of me.

It is hard to unlearn what you already know.

Money, affluence, and systemic control put Katie in the place of leadership, not competence and influence. She didn't attain that position because the people beneath her in the organization aligned with her personally or believed she was the best to steer the ship or chart the course. The employees are mostly marginalized people, taking it one day at a time, trying to survive in this ph♥cked up world. Don't get it twisted, the employees would be kind to Katie, and smile in her face, but to summarize the words of the 1971 song *Smiling Faces Sometimes* by the Temptations, smiling faces tell lies.

And, just to spit in her coffee…poor Katie. She thinks she is a leader, sitting in a chief position, aspiring to fill the large shoes of her powerful and influential parents. Katie's leadership style, however, was a disappointment. Her insecurity and resistance to constructive feedback never earned her the reverence and respect her parents once held in the community. Despite her affluence, she had little to no influence on the audience she claimed to serve.

The arrogance and ignorance of White privilege, classism, and ego clearly defines Katie. I am sure some of you know people just like Katie.

My belief in a world of rainbows and unicorns, where people are inherently good, was shattered. It didn't help me identify the situations that unfolded right in front of me years ago in that position with Goliath, nor in the experience described above.

I was oblivious to the systems of power, influence, and control that were established and circulating around me. My assumption that people are inherently good outweighed my ability to see people of privilege and influence form natural gravitation towards one another to become a united force to take me out. I even had a sorority sister, a board member, participate in manipulating the narrative that led me to part ways with FTM.

I thought to myself, as smart as I am, how in the world did I not see that coming?

There are times in life when you must take a step back and assess a situation.

Months after leaving FTM, I was forced to look within to have a better understanding of why I allowed the lack of integrity and leadership at FTM to hijack me the way it had. There were so many thoughts and feelings processed, and while it seemed very easy to blame someone else for the position I was in, I had to accept the fact that I am the only person responsible.

It may seem easy to blame someone else for where you are, but you must accept the fact that you are the only person
responsible for where you are today.

Months after taking the PI assessment for the NBA team and reflecting upon my experiences in corporate America, I now understood how I showed up in corporate America. It dawned on me that I really am a maverick! My mother wasn't the first maverick in my family. My biological father was, and I inherently am one too because it's in my DNA!

I met my biological father when I was 17 years old. He was the first Black maverick in my family. Whether I was raised by him or not, his DNA flows through me. This past February, I was asked to contribute to my company's Black History Month discussion. One of the questions was, "What historical Black figure has inspired you and why?" It was easy for me to identify and reflect upon the action my biological father took back in the 1980's.

In 1984, less than a few weeks into his job as a delivery driver for a national pizza chain, my biological father was fired from his job for refusing to shave his beard. His refusal wasn't rebellious in nature but due to a medical condition. You see, as a Black man, he suffered from a condition called pseudofolliculitis barae (PFB), a condition primarily affecting Black men. PFB occurs when highly curved hair grows back into the skin, causing inflammation and sometimes pain.

According to case law, my biological father was fired because he refused to shave his beard. He refused to allow others to place him in a box because that box could have had debilitating consequences for him. This was the 1980's, just a decade and a half after the Civil Rights Act of 1964 was passed, and my father was ready for the battle and the journey for equality. The Equal Employment Opportunity Commission joined my father in his fight and a decade later, the 8[11] U.S. Circuit Court of Appeals agreed with my father and issued their decision, citing the company did in fact have discriminatory practices.

Let That Shit Go!

I am proud that I got the maverick gene not only my biological father, but also my mother!

I spent years internalizing and expressing to others the frustration of feeling discriminated against because I am Black. I felt mistreated by others because of the color of my skin and the regurgitated narratives and stereotypes of the Black community. I have a range of emotions, anger, resentment, and sadness. I have also held on to unforgiveness entirely too long. However, last January, I changed my perspective when Laisha said, "Mom, you need to let that shit go!"

Lessons Learned

- If you are a maverick, you weren't designed to fit in.

- You shouldn't want anything that wasn't designed just for you.

- Just because you can, doesn't mean you should. It could be a costly lesson.

- It doesn't matter if they are wrong, it may or may not be worth the fight. Consider your choices wisely.

- Everything you want to say doesn't have to come out of your mouth, learn to edit yourself.

- You must own where you are in your career.

- As you climb those ladders, remember chutes and shit will come at any time.

- Learn to let the anger go.

Let That Shit Go!

O h how proud I am of Laisha! Not only did she survive my ph♥cked up parenting, but she also embraced a calling to invest in others and is such a wise and grounded young woman.

As the conversation continued, I was still grappling with my ph♥cked up personal experience with FTM and the insidious nature of White privilege. The emotional weight of the issue was heavy, and I felt compelled to speak out, to take action. See something. Say something. Right? Yet, Laisha continued to redirect my energy. She said, "Mom, why do you think it's your responsibility to save everyone else?"

I responded by saying, "Because I was placed in a position of knowing better."

She said, "Just because you know something, it doesn't mean that it is your responsibility to do something about it." Did she just paraphrase my own words? Just because you can, doesn't mean you should!

> # It is not your responsibility to save everyone else.

In my quest and pursuit of being the best version of me, I took on the internal weight of how other people's decisions created a negative impact on others, often acutely affecting marginalized people and minorities. The weight was often heavy, and the pursuit of justice was an uphill climb that one person would never be able to solve alone. I used to take that weight as motivation and fuel to spark my next move. However, my daughter was teaching me that it's okay to not pick up that weight.

Young people may not be known for being wise, but sometimes they just might surprise you. I am grateful for the relationships with my children, the ones that allow them to provide me with candid and transparent feedback. All three of my children have told me about myself in one way or another over the years. And all of them telling me about myself was delivered in love and received with an understanding that I know I am not perfect and will always be open to hearing the truth to fuel my continued growth. In a nutshell, when we stop growing, we wither, and we die.

> # It is okay to NOT pick up that weight!

I have found myself frequently reaching out to my children, seeking feedback. Over the last year, Laisha and I have embarked upon a journey of tough conversations, riddled with hurt feelings and moments of deep reflection, yet encompassed in love. I am so grateful for her courage and confidence to tell it like it is, from her perspective, because this has strengthened our relationship.

One time, she called me to share her insight and perspective as to why she thinks I view the world the way I do. It had to do with my adoptive mother raising me with blinders, her attempt to bestow upon me White privilege. She told me that the way Grandma raised me is the reason why I don't see racism for what it is. And that I see things from a jaded perspective.

During a later conversation, she asked me why I was so angry so often. My anger showed up a lot when I was raising her. Maybe it was because I felt so lost, alone, and misunderstood. Maybe it was because I was navigating this world blindly, even as a teen mom and child myself. Whatever the reason for my anger and unfortunately, whether I thought I masked it well or not, I hadn't. She received the brunt of my aggression as my first-born child. In a space of offering forgiveness and grace towards me, she asked me to take some time during my 50th birthday vacation to take a deep look inward and identify why I was so angry.

> # Learning to let go is a process.

It didn't take long for me to follow her advice. The same day she gave me the feedback, I immediately reflected on why I harbored so much hurt, anger, and resentment towards others. This revelation, along with understanding the reasons for my anger, were defining moments for this book. Understanding how my belief systems have shaped me, the need to seek feedback from others for personal growth and development and learning to let shit go.

The deliberate attempt by my adoptive mother to instill White privilege and thwart what would inherently apply to me, systemic racism as a Black woman, failed. Despite being raised in a middle-class White family and community, White privilege was not gifted upon me. It has taken me years to grasp the totality of what Robin DiAngelo describes in her book, *White Fragility*[9], about racial hierarchies and systems of power and control. But I am now WOKE!

Despite my feeling of empowerment and the ability to take on any challenge presented to me, I refuse to attribute these characteristics to my family belief system or environment, but rather, I give all praise to God. I have had to learn to navigate this ph♥cked up world alone. The Bible says when your father and mother forsake you, the Lord will lift you up, so all honor and glory I give are to God.

Learning to let go is a process. One can't go from harboring resentment and frustration to immediate liberation overnight. It is a journey for us all. It may look different for each of us, but the process of forgiveness and moving on is absolutely required to foster much needed internal healing and growth.

It's Just a Job

Letting go required me to recognize a profound truth - my career is *just a job*. I have always said that people need money just like they need oxygen. Money is required to live. Therefore, people need a job to obtain money to survive. Many get caught up, as I did, in the corporate ladder climb, only to be hit with the many different chutes - chutes that were designed to ensure we would fail to achieve a level of status reserved for the affluent and wealthy, in systems invented for people other than me.

I operated under the assumption that I could achieve the great American Dream, only to meet the brick walls designed to keep me in my place. For most of my life, I have been climbing ladders, striving to achieve something; however, defining that something has recently changed for me, opening up a new horizon of possibilities.

I have earned a lot of money and been afforded the opportunity to travel frequently to experience things in life that many people haven't even considered. Yet, my salary and adventures would appear trivial to the wealthy and affluent. My measurement of success used to be achieving that title, responsibilities, and recognition within corporate America, a title and salary demonstrating that I have arrived. But, arrived where? In a place where I was constantly stressed, where my relationships suffered, and where I felt unfulfilled, that's not the kind of 'arrival' I was striving for!

The conversations with and feedback from my children have expanded my perspective on what is and should be most important. After spending my children's formative years climbing, only to be later met with the destined chute, I realized the importance of investing in the development of the people most important to me, my children. While some people may think I am being too harsh on myself, as I was just a child myself, I do acknowledge and own the fact that I failed to invest in the intentional development of my children when they were young. Now that they are older, I am doing everything I can to learn from my mistakes and past decisions to ensure they have the very best version of me now, flaws and all.

Today, I chose to look at my job as just a job. It may be my chosen profession or career, but I will no longer allow the dynamics of a chaotic professional environment to dictate my priorities. I will choose to prioritize God, myself, and family and have learned the power of saying "no."

Recognize, your career is just a job.

Arriving at a particular salary or title will not generate positive memories for you and your loved ones. While money allows you to invest in creating certain family experiences, there are wonderful memories and experiences you can create with your loved ones that only cost you time.

Spending countless hours, nights, and weekends, investing in someone else's dream, is not going to further advance your personal mission and purpose in life. Companies and organizations will use you up and throw you away, and this perspective is coming from an HR professional. Think about all the people who have worked tirelessly for years for a company, even decades, only to be met with the ill-fated reduction in force memo, or your position-has-been-eliminated conversation, or your services are no longer needed verbiage.

Consider compartmentalizing your efforts, actions, and loyalty for your job to ensure you prioritize your mission and purpose. Maybe you establish a clear boundary where work is not allowed between certain hours when you get home and before bedtime. Maybe it is ensuring that one weekend day is dedicated to family time or personal wellbeing or development. By establishing clear boundaries, you can avoid burning out, improve your mental and physical health, and strengthen your relationships. You could establish a clear boundary where work is prohibited between certain hours when you get home and before bedtime. It could be ensuring that one weekend day is dedicated to family time, personal well-being, or development. Leverage that job to take you and your family to the life that you want to live.

> # Prioritize yourself because companies will use you up and throw you out like you are trash.

During a recent NCAA men's basketball final games series, I was surrounded by highly skilled, talented, and experienced Black male coaches. I listened intently as they expressed their frustrations and feelings of defeat when promotional announcements were published and socialized throughout the collegiate basketball coaching circuit. Despite decades of experience, familiarity with the student-athlete experience, and ability to relate to the highly sought after talented Black players, these men were nowhere on the radar for consideration of these highly compensated, prominent head coaching positions. These coveted positions are reserved for White men, who fall into the acceptable circle for continuity of power, influence, money, and control. According to The Institute for Diversity and Ethics in Sport[12], 24.8% of Division I men's basketball head coaches are White, while 52.4% of student-athletes are Black.

Even when Coach Dawn Staley, a Black woman, led her predominately Black women's basketball team at South Carolina to win their third National Championship, the media and narrative remained focused on a player with great skills and exceptional character who is White.

Systemic racism is real. Build a plan to navigate this ph♥cked up corporate world.

These examples of monumental challenges Black leaders face when seeking growth opportunities and recognition for their contributions to their respective crafts serve as a clear reminder that there is more work to be done for equity and inclusion. As a Black woman in leadership, I have learned to reprioritize what is important to me. My ability to influence the development of others remains the focal point of my existence, and I will ensure my availability and priority remains on my family and inner circle. Remember, self-care is not selfish, it's necessary for well-being and success.

In corporate America, entities exist to make a profit, whether it's business, industry, sports, entertainment, academia, healthcare, and even ministry. These institutions will use you up if you let them. Rather than allow them to use you up and let you go without warning or notice, I implore you to consider the following: Say no when your plate is full. Prioritize tasks that align with your values. Set clear expectations about your availability and workload.

Lessons Learned

- Systemic racism is real. Accept the facts and formulate your plan to navigate this ph♥cked up corporate world.

- Katie Ka-Boom and Mighty Mouse are everywhere.

- It is not your responsibility to become a martyr for others.

- Letting go of anger and disappointment is a process.

- Your career is just a job, learn to prioritize yourself.

- It is up to you to create a life you love living.

We All Have Trauma – Go to Therapy!

I know plenty of people who think that therapy is a waste of time, money, and energy. Often, these people think they have everything under control. They don't want or believe they need someone in their business to tell them what to do and how to do it. They have life in this ph♥cked up world all figured out. Well, maybe they do. Maybe they don't. I am confident that people who think they have figured it out are probably not living life to the fullest. They are merely existing, reacting to what life throws at them, and somehow managing to survive.

The idea that therapy is a waste of time, money, and energy couldn't be farther from the truth. As I mentioned earlier, many of us either have personal or family secrets or trauma we have experienced at some point in our lives. It's foolish to think we can fully understand our own complexities and nuances independent of outside resources. So many environmental and societal influences shape a belief system and dictate how you show up in life. We often unpack these dynamics on the people closest to us. This could be our friends, family, or loved ones, and they are not trained to help others heal from traumatic life experiences, because they may be carrying around their own baggage.

People close to us have a vested interest in our well-being and have predisposed opinions about our life situations. Therefore, seeking wisdom from a neutral person with an informed understanding of how life's challenges and rewards affect our actions and decision-making ability are vitally important.

I shared that I have been on this transformational journey over the past few years. During this last year, I made a huge consequential decision to take a deeper dive into the inner workings of me. This required that I partner with someone neutral to help me dissect and understand why I make the decisions I make and how my behavior and reactions to situations affect my ability to live the most productive and healthy life possible.

Seek wisdom from a neutral person.

Please understand that my experience with therapy didn't just begin this past year. There were a few times in my life where I had a need, where I was reaching out for help in navigating life, but I am sad to say that those resources were unable to meet me where I was and address my needs. The dynamics of my life have been so complex, I needed a licensed therapist who understood transracial adoption, teenage parenting, single parenting, religion, and so much more. I couldn't find the right therapist then, but I was willing to search again.

When seeking out a therapist this time, I explicitly looked for someone Black and preferably a woman. God saw fit to provide me with two options when I looked in my local community, using my insurance provider search function. I chose to approach the woman who was older and more experienced than the other. I knew I needed someone who not only had the clinical knowledge of how to help me, but I sought someone who had also lived a little bit more of life than I had.

When I met her, I knew we were kindred spirits. I am so grateful for her approachability, transparency, and willingness to guide me to steer the ship of my journey of self-discovery. I have spent the past year, nearly every week, meeting with her to unpack my traumas and rediscover me.

Because of You

It was October 2023, and my therapist had given me a homework assignment. She asked me to explore the undercurrent beneath the layers of my complexities by having me complete an attachment-style assessment. I was eager to learn about myself, so I jumped online and explored my options when I got home.

I took the first assessment and paid a nominal fee for my results. To my surprise, I was assigned a 75% Secure, 24% Avoidant, and 18% Anxious style. As I read my results further, I embraced a cynical disposition because the details did not align with my own self-awareness. I felt the report was biased toward presenting a positive view of healthy attachment style, and I knew that it did not reflect my life experience.   Therefore, I took another assessment.

This time, the assessment was free and administered by a research group. This report was more aligned with how I believe I show up with others and what I feel on the inside. The second report indicated I have an Anxious/Preoccupied attachment style.

This attachment style is characterized by a strong desire for closeness and intimacy, combined with a deep fear of rejection and abandonment. Below in italics is a summary of my results:

> *Individuals with an anxious attachment style often struggle with low self-esteem, feeling "less than" others and not good enough. This sense of inadequacy leads to self-sacrifice, where we prioritize the needs of others over their own, as we lack a solid sense of self. Our formative experiences may have been inconsistent, causing us to feel unworthy of love and seek constant validation from others in an effort to prove our own worth.*

That sounds just like me! Regardless of how I presented on the outside, on the inside I have felt that I was never good enough, always striving for what's next to accomplish. From being the little girl who chose to defy the rules and seek the comfort in relationships often with older men. To the young woman who chose to prioritize a relationship with a man, over the needs of my children. To now being the mature woman who has an intrinsic desire to serve others. I have mentioned that my purpose and calling in life is to pour into the development of others. I get a rush inspiring others but have found it very difficult to internalize my own worth.

> *We often find it challenging to be alone or single, with relationships and intimacy closely tied to our sense of self-worth. Our dependency on others can extend to decision-making, as we may struggle with asserting our own agency, relying on a partner to make choices for us. Though we are caring and attentive to our partner's needs, this focus can sometimes lead to our partner feeling overwhelmed or needing space.*

For the first time in my life, I am single, and I am loving it! While I have had short stints of not being in a relationship, the yearning for intimacy with a life partner previously stood at the forefront of my mind and drove my actions. I took a passive role in my past romantic relationships in the aspect of choosing to be together. If he chose me, I would become attached.

> *A fear of rejection or criticism can cause us to become upset over even minor disapproval, and we may be excessively vigilant in monitoring our relationships for signs of threat, often misinterpreting situations. This can lead to clingy or needy behavior, especially if our partner seeks time outside of the relationship, often triggering jealousy and frustration. Despite our caring nature, our*

tendency to overanalyze and misread relational dynamics can complicate their connections.

I can't even count the number of times I acted as a complete fool in my relationships when I was younger, due to insecurity and fear of betrayal. I went from jumping down a flight of stairs with my fist cocked back, ready to bust my boyfriend in the face in high school and breaking my foot to later breaking into another one of my boyfriend's college dorm room. I was an absolute hot mess. From this foolish behavior, I graduated into a full-fledged inspector. I would drive around neighborhoods in the middle of the night, fueled by a compulsive need to prove that he was out there doing something he wasn't supposed to be doing. Have you ever heard, *you are what you attract, or if you look for it, you'll find it?*

At the beginning of my most recent relationship, the guy asked me why I was still single. My response to him was that I was picky, and my expectations of men were so high. He immediately pushed back and said something to the effect of your standards aren't that high if your ex is exactly as you described him. It was at that moment; I had to pause and consider the narrative I was telling myself.

I was telling myself that they were the problem, but in reality, I was. I had little to no standards, and he could see that. I'm incredibly thankful for his honesty and transparency. If he hadn't pointed that out, I might still be living in a fantasy, thinking that I wasn't a major factor in why I had not built a healthy, sustainable relationship with a man. I had a bad picker and needed to better understand why.

As I continued to explore my attachment style, I unearthed the foundation on which my style was built. I was drawn to the book of Jeremiah. Jeremiah 1:5 says, "Before I formed you in the womb, I knew you", my attachment style began developing in the womb.

I believe, in the womb, I could hear her voice. I had a sense of safety, warmth, and protection. For more than 270 days, while I was forming and developing, we established a connection, a bond. A bond so miraculous, unique, and undeniably powerful, it cannot be duplicated or replaced. For 9 months, while I was in her womb, the bond established with her was the foundation for my existence and emotional wellbeing.

The day was near, and I was ready to meet the world, her world. As she pushed through her labor pains, she finally held me in her arms. I could feel her touch; I could smell her; she was safe, comfortable, familiar, and all I had ever known. I was now in her world, in her loving arms. For a few days, she embraced, held, and loved me. Until that day…

Ripped from the only place of comfort, peace, and safety, separated from the only human connection I had, I was thrust into a fight or flight response at just a few days old. I entered an unfamiliar world in distress and despair. She chose to place me up for adoption.

Studies indicate that when a baby is placed for adoption, both emotional and physiological changes can occur, although the extent of these effects can vary.

Emotional & Physiological Effects on the Baby:

Stress Response: Babies, like adults, have a physiological stress response. When separated from their birth mother, the baby may experience elevated levels of cortisol, a stress hormone, which can affect their mood, sleep, and general wellbeing.

Separation Anxiety: Although newborns don't have fully developed cognitive awareness, they still experience discomfort and distress from the sudden absence of the familiar sounds, smells, and sensations associated with their birth mother.

Trust and Security Issues: A baby's sense of trust is rooted in their early experiences with caregivers. If the separation from their birth mother is abrupt or traumatic, it may lead to difficulties in forming trust and secure attachments in the future, potentially resulting in anxiety or emotional challenges.

Grief and Loss: Even though babies may not have conscious memory of their early experiences, they can still feel the effects of early separation. As they grow, feelings of loss and abandonment may surface in various forms as they develop a sense of self and attachment.

Attachment and Bonding:

> **Attachment Formation**: The early bonding experience with the birth mother is crucial for a baby's emotional development. Being placed for adoption may disrupt the initial attachment process.

> **Attachment disruption:** A baby may experience initial disruption in attachment when separated from their birth mother. The baby might feel insecure or anxious, especially if the adoption process involves sudden separation.

> **New attachment formation:** As the baby bonds with the adoptive parents over time, they begin to form a new attachment. With consistent care, comfort, and affection, the baby can develop a secure attachment to their new caregivers.

Babies may have difficulty forming secure attachments due to the separation from their birth parents. This can lead to challenges in building trust and forming healthy relationships as they grow.

Impact of Adoption on Development: In some cases, adopted children may experience a heightened sense of being "different," particularly if they are aware of their adoption status. This could manifest emotionally as they navigate questions about identity and belonging, and they may experience feelings of being displaced or disconnected, particularly in adolescence.

Questions of Identity and Self-Worth: Adopted children may struggle with questions about their identity and self-esteem. They may wonder about their birth parents or the reasons for their adoption, which can influence their sense of self.

Behavioral Concerns: Some adopted children may display behavioral issues, such as aggression, defiance, or difficulty reading social cues. These behaviors can often be linked to past trauma and the difficulties of adapting to a new family dynamic.

Increased Anxiety and Depression: Adopted children are more likely to experience anxiety and depression. The trauma of being separated from their birth family and adjusting to a new environment can contribute to these emotional struggles.

The exploration into my attachment style led me down a path of pain, heartache, and discovery into thoughts and feelings I suppressed and ignored for years. It proved to align with my Ph❤ckIt! attitude, I can't do anything about that, pick up the pieces and push on.

 I identified a common theme when dissecting my behavior patterns and the choices I made throughout my life. My choices have been impacted by the physiological reactions I have towards stress. The constant fight or flight has shown up in my ability to self-regulate and follow the rules as a child. I had poor personal boundaries and sought comfort from inappropriate relationships with older men.

Over the years I have had health problems with digestion and sleep patterns. I am a self-proclaimed, selectively social introvert. Earlier in the book I shared that I really don't like being around others. Thank God, I didn't follow the path of other family members with illicit substance abuse, but I do have a few things I struggle to let go of.

Shortly after taking the assessment, the song *Because of You* by Kelly Clarkson played in the background. I always loved that song, because when I first heard it 20 years ago, it helped me realize I was not alone. There was someone else who felt the pain and agony of growing up or living in a chaotic and dysfunctional environment.

The song describes the influence and effects of one person's actions, and how they manifest emotionally and psychologically in the other person. Choices, regardless of intent, have consequences.

For many years, I imagined singing Kelly Clarkson's song to my biological mother. I have harbored a great deal of pain, anger, frustration, and resentment due to the deeply invasive feelings of rejection and unworthiness. She made a choice to have consensual sex, carry a fetus to term, and give birth to me. I didn't choose to be here in this life. A choice was made for me.

I shared the emotional and physiological effects on me, the baby, but I also want to recognize that there are long lasting effects for my biological mother.

Emotional and Physiological Effects on Birth Mothers:

For the birth mother, the emotional and physiological impact can also be profound:

Emotional Trauma and Grief: The decision to place a baby for adoption can be accompanied by a deep sense of grief, loss, and sadness. This emotional pain can be exacerbated by hormonal shifts, as the mother's body adjusts after childbirth. There may be feelings of guilt, shame, or a sense of sacrifice.

Hormonal Responses: After childbirth, the birth mother's body undergoes hormonal changes as it transitions out of the postpartum period. The drop in hormones like oxytocin (associated with bonding and nurturing) can contribute to feelings of sadness, loss, or depression.

Psychological Impact: In the long term, a birth mother may experience challenges related to attachment, identity, or even societal judgment. The emotional effects of placing a child for adoption can last a lifetime.

I also mentioned earlier that I met my biological father at the age of 17. I also met my biological mother at the age of 21. Our first few meetings were superficial in nature, as I didn't have a strong interest in getting to know her. I was young, self-absorbed, and focused on defining a life for myself and my two children.

At that time, I was consciously more interested in developing a relationship with my biological father, a Black man, than developing a relationship with my biological mother, a White woman. I embraced my identity as a Black woman and knew the world would forever see me as a Black person, so my interest in exploring a relationship with my biological father's family was my only interest at that time.

I spent almost all of the next 30 years of my life without a relationship with my biological mother.

Today, I understand she did what she believed was best for me, but she has no idea how her singular choice negatively impacted my life. The imminent stress of losing everything familiar created a perpetual and pervasive effect on me.

I also imagined signing that song to my adoptive parents,

because I felt they didn't stop and take the time to intentionally prepare me for what this ph♥cked up world was going to show me as a Black woman. But how could they really know how to prepare me for my Blackness? I now recognize that they couldn't because they weren't like me.

The feelings of resentment towards my parents resonated with me so strongly that the anger and frustration I felt towards them showed up in how I parented my children.

I wrote about generational curses and the patterns of negative behaviors and emotional challenges that are passed down through generations. My unchecked, undealt with trauma and ignorance perpetuated relationship struggles, an inability to self-regulate when emotionally hijacked, and the failure to establish healthy boundaries within my children. Were my choices and actions intentional? In some cases, yes, but it is essential to understand that the answer is no in many situations. It's not always a conscious decision but a result of the patterns we've inherited.

I take ownership and accountability for the atmosphere I set for my children. Just as you must take ownership and accountability for the atmosphere you create for your family. The purpose of my writing is to create an atmosphere of vulnerability, to bear the intimate details of my upbringing, life experiences, and lessons I've learned along the way to help others understand how our choices impact our lives.

I'm reminded again of the important role music has played in my life. Music has always served as an escape for me. I'm known for listening to the same song over and over again. I've often said that music, especially instrumental music, can take you to anywhere you want to go.

When I was younger, I didn't realize that my music choices influenced my decisions. Have you heard the expression; *you are what you hear, see, and do*?

When I listened to love music, I was eager to replicate what was in the song into my relationships. It didn't matter whether there was any applicable truth to the lyrics in the song, if I was singing about it, I was manifesting that feeling into my life.

Songs like "*All of Me*" by John Legend inspired me to accept my partner with flaws and all (regardless of how bad those damn flaws were!) "*By Your Side*", by Sade influenced me to showcase just how loyal I could be, without regard for what I was receiving in return. I would imagine my man signing me songs like "*If This World Were Mine*" by Luther Vandross, and those jokers weren't the least bit thinking about giving me the world. But the frequent and consistent playing of love music invaded my mind so much, I was left with the impression that this was the type of relationship we were living in.

If I listened to songs like "*Irreplaceable*" by Beyonce, "*Before He Cheats*" by Carrie Underwood, or "*Can't Raise a Man*" by K. Michelle, my insecurities would be magnified, and I would find myself searching for examples in real life to address with my man. If you look for it, you will find it!

While I embraced growing up with hip-hop and singing the tunes of Salt-N-Pepa, Snoop Dogg, N.W.A., Eminem, and MC Breed, it was the therapeutic sounds of Cece Winans and Yolanda Adams that provided the inspiration I needed to keep moving forward.

What we listen to has a direct impact on our feelings and thoughts. Music has a profound impact on our emotions, shaping how we feel and processing life's experiences.

Through its lyrics and melodies, music offers a powerful outlet for emotional release and expression, helping us articulate and release complex emotions. Our emotional response to music provides a sense of healing, allowing us to process difficult experiences and visualize personal transformation. Whether through uplifting tunes that inspire hope or calming rhythms that ease anxiety, music can regulate moods and offer a safe space for emotional exploration and stability.

Beyond emotional healing, music also connects us to memories and experiences, triggering vivid recollections that evoke deep feelings. These memories, tied to the lyrics or melodies, can be both comforting and enlightening, offering us a sense of connection to our past and providing solace during tough times.

Music has physical healing properties, including reducing stress and enhancing overall well-being. In therapeutic settings, it is often used to promote relaxation, lower blood pressure, and support the body's natural healing processes. I can listen to Boney James and Kenny G. all day long, when I need to detach, decompress and re-center myself.

Music also serves as a source of inspiration and motivation, encouraging self-reflection, perseverance, and personal growth. "*Alabaster Box*" by Cece Winans was one of the first spiritual songs that spoke to the depths of my soul. Every time I play that song; I am brought to a place of deep gratitude and worship. I get stopped in my tracks to reflect on just how good God has been towards me.

We don't know the cost for each person's journey in this life. We don't know the trials and the ph♥cked up trauma that another has experienced that have shaped them into the person they are today. We need to show one another kindness, compassion, tolerance, grace, and forgiveness.

Psalm 27:10 says "*When my father and my mother forsake me, the Lord will take me up.*" (KJV)

The Love of Jesus

I didn't grow up in a religious household, but in my early teens, I found myself wrapped in the loving arms of Jesus. After the birth of Laisha, at the age of 16, I discovered a love like no other. I was at a point in life where I was contemplating suicide. I didn't know how to be a parent; I didn't know how to navigate life; I was a lost little girl with a baby to raise. I felt completely alone and misunderstood. The thought of drinking a soda laced with poison, and providing the same concoction to Laisha, seemed to be the best move to make.

But God arrested my spirit and locked me up into a relationship with Him.

> # God will arrest your spirit to lock you up in a relationship with Him!

God saw fit, to use Laisha's paternal grandmother and uncle, to encourage and help me see life through a different lens. It was after this encounter that I chose to seek a local ministry to strengthen me in my very vulnerable and fragile state. The house of God, and a relationship with God, was what my soul and spirit so desperately needed. I needed to feel wanted, included, valued, and loved. It was in this space where I transformed my codependency in bad relationships, into the co-dependency in and with God.

Often as babies in Christ, or people who are new in their walk with God, we come to church in some of the most broken stages of our lives seeking wisdom and guidance. People in leadership positions in ministry have a difficult role to play in the lives of believers, especially young believers, or babies in Christ. We are open and vulnerable, many times very weak, placing our trust in leaders in ministry. This weakened and vulnerable state of being creates a ripe atmosphere for people in power to exercise manipulation, dominance, and control.

A church, a ministry, a place of worship, or house of God is intended to be a place of refuge, a sanctuary, or a safe place for people to go to be uplifted and given hope for better days. In the biblical teachings and Christian principles, I also learned lessons about discernment between God and man. I learned that even though a person is a minister, even though they have a calling from God to teach, develop, and guide others, they, too, are human, and they, too, are flawed, and they, too, make mistakes.

> # Ministers, Pastors, and Preachers are flawed and make mistakes too!

Be careful who you allow close to your spirit and soul. Not everyone in ministry is sent by God, and not everyone in ministry has your best interest at heart. As I stated earlier, even ministries are a business, many are in it to be profitable. Don't let anyone tell you churches or ministries are only designed for the further advancement of people's spiritual lives. Church is a business, designed to make money, and while many churches and ministries reinvest right back into their church and/or communities, others do not. And these are the ministries I urge you to steer away from.

The Bible says you know the tree by the fruit it bears. Study the church/ministry you are affiliated with or are considering affiliation with:

- What are the founding principles and belief systems?
- What type of legacy or community influence does it have?
- Does it bear fruit? What type of fruit does it bear?
    - Sweet Fruit
        - A positive brand in the community.
        - Membership is growing.
        - Members are friendly and approachable.
        - Leaders are responsive to your inquiries.
        - You see examples of relationships you would aspire to have.
    - Bitter Fruit
        - Membership is dwindling or stagnant.
        - Members are unapproachable and/or rude.
        - Inquiries go unanswered.
        - Lack of role models/examples to follow.

These are just a few examples for you to consider when choosing an affiliation.

What I appreciate about the ministry that birthed my spiritual journey is that it helped define the foundation of my spiritual belief system, one that is rooted in the Word of God. Regardless of what a person was teaching, I was taught to seek the Word of God for myself, to study to show thyself approved. Thank you, Bishop B, for laying the spiritual foundation that has carried me through the years.

Throughout my walk with God and getting to know His promises through the love of Jesus, I encountered so many people who would tell me to take my problems to God. God, as the omnipresent, all-knowing, all-powerful God, can solve all my problems. I tried that for a while, going to church upwards of 5 times a week.

Faith is an action word. You cannot expect God to work things out for you, if you are not willing to do the work.

Listening to praise and worship music uplifted and helped me during difficult times. An all-time favorite is "*Never Give Up*" by Yolanda Adams. That woman knows she can sing! Her words of encouragement and inspiration were on repeat for years. It wasn't until I got all learned up and realized that faith without works is dead!

I cannot expect God to work things out for my good when I am not willing to put in the work. Faith is *an action word* that requires action from the believer. While I am not going to quote a bunch of scriptures, because I can't remember them all, they are hidden in my heart, as guiding principles. The scripture tells me that if it is going to work, I am going to have to work it. I must then allow the Holy Spirit to guide me along the way.

> # While church and ministries offer spiritual growth, they should not replace therapy.

This is why I strongly believe that you should seek therapy outside of the church. Now, if there is a licensed professional therapist/counselor who happens to go to your church, great! Connect with that person, but please, don't seek therapy from a non-clinical, non-licensed individual, because all they can offer you is advice, not wisdom as learned from a trained and hands-on education.

As the all-knowing, all-yielding, powerful God we know He is, He created the curriculum, degrees, and licensures for practicing clinicians. Let them operate in their gift and calling in order to help you best operate in yours.

Finding the Right One

I tried finding therapy multiple times, but I concluded that it either wasn't the right time or place, because surely, I know it wasn't the right therapist. As a gifted and talented Black maverick, I have found myself telling my life story to therapists, only for them to look at me with admiration and disbelief that I had made it thus far. Wait – what? I am coming to you for help, and you want to praise me? I don't understand.

I remember after a few sessions with one lady, I just stopped going back. I was in my early 30's and she just sat there, listening to me in amazement. I was like – "Look, lady – I need *help*, and the respect and admiration of me for how far I've come isn't helping me understand how to navigate these challenges." I should have known. She was a White woman, and we were in the South, so she maybe hadn't seen a progressive Black woman.

Remember how I shared the importance of finding mentors? I tend to look at people who have more experience in areas that I am less familiar with to learn from in all aspects of life. Over the years, I learned so much more from friends and family members who became mentors in my transformational journey than I did from those therapists.

In the space of therapy, I learned to lean on my sister, Jami who has been in and out of therapy for years. What I appreciate and respect about Jami's journey is that despite the cards being stacked against her, she has overcome major obstacles such as the feelings of rejection from family as well as addiction to a typically lethal drug. As a proud mother, wife, friend, and sister, I am proud to look at my sister as my mentor in many spaces, not just therapy.

For most of my life, the trauma of being separated from my birth mother and the resulting constant state of fight-or-flight has caused significant memory gaps from my early childhood. This prolonged stress response disrupted my brain's ability to form and retain memories, leading to a fragmented recollection of events before the age of 10. When I speak to groups and share my story, I share that most memories I can recall come only when prompted by a visual reminder or photograph. Even then, I struggle to recall certain details. I have learned that often people block out traumatic events, in an attempt for self-preservation and protection.

In my therapeutic journey and with my inability to recall certain life events, I have found the need to connect with Jami, as she knows me in some ways better than I know myself.

As my older sister, she was the one who would babysit me and my brother when we were young when our parents would go out. She was always there for me while growing up and is always the one to help me remember the positive memories, despite the overwhelming magnification I place on the negative ones.

I remember many years ago, I was struggling emotionally and during a phone call, I told her I don't remember my childhood. I was crying, saddened by the fact that there are very few memories I can recall. That year, at Christmas, she provided me with the most beautiful gift. She put together a photo album of me when I was a baby, toddler, and in my younger years.

Accompanied by the photo album was a card. In the card, she wrote that she remembers how much I was loved and how fun it was to watch and see me grow over the years. She was so thoughtful, deliberate, and intentional by taking the time to show me she heard my cries for help. She wanted to do something to lessen the pain I was in. I love her so much and am grateful for her selfless acts of continual love.

Another set of mentors who have been significant in my therapeutic journey are my children. I have leaned heavily on my daughters to assist me in my journey in therapy. All three of my children have been instrumental in helping me become more self-aware, accepting, and forgiving.

Laisha is the first one in our family to take a deep dive into therapy and begin the work for her journey towards healing. While this isn't my story to tell, I will say that she was having a tough time and in a dark space. Through the love and support from her bonus mom, she was introduced to a therapist who began helping her process her emotions and feelings by providing her with the necessary tools and support.

At that time in my life, I was still busy trying to save everyone else around me and hadn't slowed down enough to realize the work I needed for myself. However, I was extremely supportive of Laisha's decision to go to therapy and encouraged her to work on strengthening her relationship with God.

Over the months and years, I recall times when she would tell me, "I love you, Mom, but I can't talk to you right now." I respected her boundaries while not fully understanding her frame of reference. After time had passed, she was able to open up to me and share how some of the work she was doing in therapy surfaced feelings she needed space and time to process. Let me tell you, some of the times she opened up to me and shared her feelings hurt me to my core. There were times that my behavior impacted her in ways I failed to understand over the years, and I was devastated.

When I finally understood and processed Laisha's feedback, I apologized for my behavior and its consequential impact and made a promise to her. The promise is to give her and her siblings the best version of me in every interaction moving forward - to be the mom, she and the others need me to be.

Throughout her journey, I have observed her transformation and have so much respect for her. Time and time again, she has shared nuggets of wisdom with me, that she picked up on her journey.

I hadn't created an atmosphere for my children to speak up and share their thoughts and feelings with me, especially if the feedback was related to something I had done wrong. It wasn't until I was much older when Laisha told me, "*Mom, you know Kylie isn't you.*" It was at that moment that I had to stop to process and understand what she was saying.

Your children should be able to give you feedback.

Kylie was in high school at the time and having fun. My traumatic adolescent years made me believe that Kylie was out there doing the very things I had done in my teenage years, but she wasn't. Kylie had developed her own set of core values and belief system. Kylie had a foundation and belief that she could accomplish anything she wanted, and that was not contingent upon a relationship.

This single comment helped me realize that your children should be able to give you feedback. They know you from a lens that only they understand, and if you value the relationship with them, you may want to open yourself up to feedback from them. I am so proud of her for being the first in our family to invest in herself. She forged the path for the rest of us to follow.

Like her older sister, Kylie began her journey in therapy well before I did. While she lives life to the fullest capacity, every waking moment of her life, she, too, suffers from traumatic experiences that have shaped her emotional well-being. As a young woman dedicated to being the best version of herself, at the age of 22, an architecture student, she frequently invests in her personal development by reading self-help books, listening to positive affirmation podcasts to develop positive coping mechanisms to improve her quality of life.

Over the years, I have witnessed how she listens intently to understand unique perspectives and displays empathy, compassion, and kindness. Her resilience in the face of adversity is admirable. Not only is Kylie a student athlete and leader on her basketball team, but she is also the coach of a youth basketball team, has her own clothing brand, and makes music. I sometimes sit back and wonder, who is this young lady? How did she become so wise? "She is an old soul," my sister professed just a few days after she was born.

In her caring and compassionate way, Kylie, too, has offered me so much advice over the years. I find myself reaching out to her on certain topics, just to hear her validate my sentiments and in some instances, guide and redirect me to see things from an alternative perspective.

At 21, she was reading Brian Tracy's, *No Excuses: The Power of Self-Discipline*[13], and told me I needed to read it, too. I did. By reading this book, I was sending a positive reinforcing message to Kylie, that I accept and appreciate her feedback. I am not sure if she knows how this book reignited me taking personal accountability for my life.

Because I have been open and honest with my children, Kylie provided me with a beautiful gift a few years ago. As mentioned earlier, she listened intently and heard what I was saying during our conversations. She knew I was on a journey of self-discovery and transformation. For Christmas, she gifted me a mug with the inscription, "Sometimes you forget you're awesome, so this is your reminder," and *The Pivot Year*[14] by Brianna Wiest, with 365 short stories of inspiration and guidance in making decisions to change and alter your life's trajectory.

My daughters were setting an example for me, the parent, to follow as it relates to therapy and finding the help I needed. But it wasn't until this book was completely written and submitted to the editor, that I learned yet another lesson from my children, and this time it was from my son, Jamal.

I thought Jamal's arrest in 2018 was going to kill me. The depth of pain I felt disrupted my equilibrium. My one and only son suffered for years with emotional and psychological trauma, due to generational curses and my divorce from his father. His pain led to substance abuse. His substance abuse led him down a path of self-destruction. Now, he was no longer in physical reach. I wouldn't be able to hug him, see his smile, feel his joyful presence, or protect him from himself or this ph♥cked up world that places a target on the back of every Black man in America.

Low and behold, it wasn't Jamal's actual arrest that nearly killed me, it was how I handled his release from prison seven years later.

The excitement had been building for years, months, and then days. My son was coming home! To complicate my life even further, I decided to relocate from Omaha back to the Dallas area during the same month he was going to be released. Jamal was incarcerated in Arizona, and while I considered moving back to Arizona, I chose Dallas for me and my quality of life. Here I go again making decisions without fully thinking things through.

While I attempted to assist with the interstate compact process, which would allow him to transfer his probation from Arizona to Texas, the timing and process became daunting, cumbersome, and totally out of my control.

When he was released, we were all there for him. His dad, his sister, his brother (on his dad's side), and me. We couldn't wait to see him, hug him, cry with him, and of course love on him.

His story is not my story to tell, so I will only tell you what I experienced the 3-4 months following his release from prison. As a parent, I wanted to do everything I possibly could to make up for lost time, help my son find his way, and assist him in creating a plan for the next phase of his life. I was willing and able to pour into him financially, emotionally, and spiritually.

However, that came to a screeching halt one day, when I realized that I could no longer pour from an empty cup. I was at the end of my rope; I couldn't see the forest for the trees. I became hyper-focused on controlling every aspect of his life that I didn't realize I was losing my own mind.

In a state of panic, I aborted everything important in my life and took a leave of absence. I took a leave of absence from my job, from my relationship, and from every other distraction thrown my way. I realized that if I wanted a different experience in life, one beyond the endless cycle of ups and downs, I had to make a change. I needed help, and I needed more therapy.

I frantically searched for a new therapist because I knew I couldn't be okay alone. I needed help, and I needed it fast. I was determined to explore multiple options. I didn't want to limit myself to the belief that I only needed one therapist for my journey. I started the interview process with Psychology Today, which was the best resource for finding therapists in my area. I made appointments with four to five and ended up seeing two regularly. I also found a psychiatrist.

As I sat in silence, I marinated on the helplessness that I felt. I didn't want to lose my son again. I wanted him to be healthy, happy, and safe, but he was so far away from me physically and I didn't know what to do.

I think this was God's way of slowing me down, to ensure He got the glory for what was about to take place. The guy I had been dating at the time also suggested to me over the years to slow down. He would say that I didn't need to rush to do everything so quickly. I had been in such a state of survival my entire life, I didn't know what it meant to slow down.

It was a phone call from my dear friend Marketha, a true root and lifetime branch, who had been there for me for nearly 30 years, that transformed my situation. Her relationships with others helped propel me in the direction I believe God intended for me. It was an early morning phone call, and she said, "*Carole, let me introduce you to Ms. Betty.*"

Ms. Betty is a local legend in the Addiction and Recovery community here in Dallas. Amid our conversation and me expressing my despair, she announced with such conviction that parenting a child is very different than parenting an adult child. She encouraged me to consider attending a local Families Anonymous meeting. That very night, I was in attendance.

It was no coincidence that the topic for the evening was "detachment." God knew exactly what He was doing! A few days prior, my therapist was talking to me about learning to detach from unhealthy situations and relationships and the importance of self-care.

Listening to the others in the meeting helped me once again realize I was not alone. Others had experienced the sleepless nights, the feelings of hopelessness, but had also learned how to conjure up the strength and courage to make new choices.

God was showing me that no matter how dark it gets, He is still in control and has a plan to work it all out. I was inspired to see my situation from a fresh perspective. I too could make different choices, if I wanted different outcomes. Even if that meant I had to show up differently for Jamal.

That evening, I learned as a parent, when we intervene to solve problems for our children, we rob them of the gift to learn the lessons for themselves. Now, this doesn't always apply when we are talking about young children, but with adult children, this absolutely must apply. We must learn to give our adult children the gift of making their own decisions and accepting the consequences of those decisions.

While I didn't get a gold star or the blue ribbon of parenting through immediate detachment and self-empowerment, I was able to take steps forward in releasing Jamal back over to God.

When God allowed Jamal to be arrested back in 2018, I knew it was God's way of protecting him from himself. Five years ago, when God said just because you can, doesn't mean you should, was manifesting its relevance again this day. Just because I can help my son, doesn't mean I should. If I do intervene, would I be robbing him of the gift of learning a life lesson?

I eventually learned to detach from trying to save my son from himself. I must remind myself somedays how important it is to allow others to learn from their decisions. When I learned to let go of Jamal, Jamal's journey of growth began.

My son eventually made it to Texas and immediately connected with a therapist and is receiving therapy and psychiatric help. It hasn't been all rainbows and unicorns since his arrival. We've had some knock-down, drag-out conversations, and there are still years of trauma we both need to work through.

> # When parents try to solve adult children's problems, we are robbing them of the gift of learning life's lessons.

But God! My son got baptized in November 2024 and renewed his relationship with God. The intrinsic drive to succeed is deeply rooted in my children and me, and my son is no exception. Despite the multiple odds stacked against him, his willpower to be great will always shine through the darkest of days.

I am so proud of who my son is and who he is becoming. With the assistance of his dad's community relationships, he was accepted in and currently enrolled in Paul Quinn College, a local HBCU. While his passion is making music, his desire is to obtain a degree in Math and work in the field of business analytics. He is so smart, gifted and talented. I am so proud of the choices he has made.

I am eternally grateful to my children for loving me enough to provide me with the gift of feedback. I am because of them, and they are because of me. ♥

Going Back to the Beginning

In the spring of 2024, I had the pleasure of attending a 50th birthday celebration for a childhood friend, I will call him Red. While we have remained connected via social media and held occasional conversations throughout the years, we hadn't really connected in more than 30 years. While I was excited to link up, I couldn't deny the feelings of anxiousness and nervousness, as I wondered would I really be able to connect with him and others after these many years?

Growing up on Jones Street in the 80's, we had a blast! When I say growing up, we were literally babies and toddlers when we met as neighbors. There was this group of kids, all within similar age ranges, who spent every waking hour together. While we didn't all go to the same primary schools, we spent afternoons and weekends together—swimming, parks, block parties, etc. When we got older, we ran the streets and did whatever we thought was fun. We were a committed pack of mischievous teens, wandering aimlessly throughout the neighborhood, sneaking out of the house. Where we grew up, there were tunnels that went under the main street in the city near the local university, and we loved traipsing through those tunnels in the middle of the night, just to be out of the house!

Yet, when I was in my early teens, my life choices put me in a different place than my childhood friends. My parents divorced. I moved away from Jones Street, and I am not sure if I ever really looked back, until the night of the party.

When I left my hometown nearly 25 years ago, I resolved to never return. My recollection of home was not a place of comfort and peace. The city was just a place where I was raised as I struggled to recall any positive memories. So, when I moved back home in 2023, I was conflicted when it came to opportunities for me to reconnect and engage with people I hadn't seen in years.

Before the party, I reached out to my brother, questioning if he was going to be there. He had to work. I further questioned, "Oh no, who is going to be my buffer? Who is going to help me remember people I may have forgotten?"

He told me to, "Stop it. You'll be fine; just go!" So, nervously, off to the party I went.

The party was at a local country club, and I didn't want to be late AND the only Black person in the room. My neighborhood friends were all White, so I felt it was appropriate for me to be on time. Upon arrival, I awkwardly looked for Red; he was taking photos with his family. Then, out of the corner of my eye, I saw another familiar face and navigated towards Justin.

After a brief introduction to Justin's girlfriend and a few others, I found myself sitting at the table with Red's family. His mother, sisters, aunts, and cousins, they all remembered me, and I was struggling to remember their names. Has it really been more than 30 years? As the conversations progressed and memories were shared, I saw other familiar faces joining the party.

I spent the next 30 minutes anchored to a select few individuals who made me feel welcomed, remembered, and valued, all the while pointing out others, I should have remembered but didn't. I pretty much giggled throughout the night and made a joke about my lack of recollection. Thankfully, everyone seemed to understand and guided me through the re-introductions.

To top off the evening, I reconnected with my first ever crush! He reminded me that he gave me neon socks in the third grade and that I was his first crush as well. What started as a birthday party turned into an elementary and middle school neighborhood reunion! So many memories, some remembered and some forgotten.

A few hours into the evening, I reconnected with one of my very best friends from middle school, inseparable at that point in our lives. I had to stop and think, when was the last time I saw her? Was it really that night we were caught sneaking out of the house and I stole my dad's car? Yes, it was. Wow! She said, "I don't think I have seen you since you were with that one guy, Laisha's dad." Yes, it had been almost 35 years.

That night, we spent the evening laughing, dancing, and talking until the country club staff just looked at us like, *really, you can go home now.* A select few took the party to Red's home, and we continued talking until four in the morning.

While sitting at his basement bar, the wife of another childhood friend began talking with me. Jackie said her husband always spoke very highly of me, but my high school reputation preceded me in a much stronger way than the words of her husband. She said there was a level of fear in her and her friends because my reputation was one of intimidation and that I would fight anyone for any reason. She also shared that she was often afraid of what might happen to her if she ran into me in a public setting without anyone else around.

I sat there, looking deep in her eyes, and I could see the genuine worry she must have felt back then. At that time, I was a very angry person, and I would fight anyone, boy or girl, if they made me mad. What I never thought about was how my identity struggle affected those around me. She also vaguely referenced that some people may still have the same impression of me today, as I hadn't been around in so long.

I sat at the bar with tears in my eyes and pain in my heart, realizing I could make someone feel so insecure, so scared to even be in my presence. She was just a child at the time, but I, too, was just a child. I have known for some time that I have an undeniable presence when I enter a room, you know, the law of

E.F. Hutton[15] – when a true leader speaks, people listen. But I had no idea I had that same presence back then and that presence was negative!

At that moment, it felt as if everyone stopped in their private conversations, and all eyes were on me. "Why are you crying? What happened? What's wrong?" another friend asked. I quickly said that nothing was wrong. I shared that Chrstina touched the very depth of my soul, and I was in awe and a space of gratitude for her sharing so openly and vulnerably. She said, "As an adult, she knew that when kids act out as I did, that there are so many deeper things happening on the inside." Wow! How did she know to target my soul like that? How is it that a friend's wife that I barely knew anything about, other than her name, was able to deliver such a powerful message to me? Maybe that was **God** speaking through Jackie!

God knows the timing of everything and the need I had, deep on the inside. Not only was Jackie looking at me that evening, but she also saw me as that broken and hurt teenage girl, way back then. In just a few sentences, her words transported me back to the defiant and reckless teenage version of me and I was revisited by the loneliness, fear, anger, and discontent I felt most of my life. With all the heaviness in the atmosphere, it was time for a break. We all headed to the backyard. While others continued laughing and talking with one another, I quietly reflected upon the enlightening conversation with Jackie and how this evening transformed my memories of home.

My childhood friends have no idea how valuable that evening was for me. The reconnection and fellowship nourished my soul. Processing through my innermost feelings in therapy has opened my spirit and soul to discovering why I feel the way I do. I'm learning how to ensure these feelings do not derail me in pursuit of my purpose and passion in life. I was welcomed home, with open arms, and seen by the ones that still loved me and were there with me from adolescence to the present.   An evening with friends allowed me to see that regardless of space and time, regardless of decisions I made that forced us into polarized spaces in life, that I, just as I am, am still valued and loved in my personal journey in this ph♥cked up world. ♥

Healing and Learning to Love Yourself is a Process

The moment you decide to unpack all your bullshit and take a deep look within; you may become worried about what you will discover. That's okay, it's a process. To heal, you must unpack what is weighing you down. Sometimes it won't readily be available in the forefront of our minds, and this will take some time. Don't pressure yourself to find healing overnight. After all, you didn't get ph♥cked up overnight. Did you?

> # Unpack your bullshit and unpack it often.

Disclaimer: I am not a therapist, and my opinion should not be considered as actions you should take. Any opinions expressed and shared are based upon my own personal awareness and experiences.

When you take a step forward and invest in your mental health, please know that the investment may become very uncomfortable, creating internal conflict as to whether it's worth the effort. Have you ever heard someone say, *when you take one step forward, you feel as though there is something trying to pull you 10 steps backwards?* Know that taking steps is momentum.

Sir Issac Newton's Third Law of Motion is known as the law of action and reaction.

According to Newton's Third Law[16], the particles exert equal and opposite forces on one another, so any change in the momentum of one particle is exactly balanced by an equal and opposite change of the momentum of another particle.

Anytime you take steps forward, there will be resistance as you leave your comfort zone of familiarity. Negative forces and energy may attack you when you start moving in the direction of your destiny. I encourage you to anticipate the attack and recognize the negative forces. Be ready for the attack and be even more ready to put on those boxing gloves, to fight for your life, and to take control of your future. You deserve a life that is not only worth living, but a life you love as the best version of yourself.

A few years ago, I read *Dare to Lead*[17] by Brene Brown. Now, I know I am not going to articulate her teachings in a skillful and deliberate manner as she did, but I am going to do my best to summarize what I took from the lesson.

A key point I recall is that when people don't have enough information about a situation, we tend to formulate stories and draw conclusions that may be false but make sense to us. We sometimes won't even ask questions to get clarification but will rather create an answer for our own narrative in our minds and run with it. How silly is this?

She says the most powerful story we tell is **the story we tell ourselves**. Now, take a moment to reflect on the stories about who you are, what you have done, what you will become, that are running through your mind. I know the stories I have told myself over the years. These were stories of doubt, insecurity, fear, failure, which were often never verbalized to another soul. Do you see the trend of negativity?

What we focus on, or what marinates in our minds, will absolutely manifest in our lives. I remember a year after giving birth to Jamal, I looked in the mirror and told myself I was fat. The following twelve months, I spent maybe only a few days in the gym all year (period) but kept repeating the narrative in my mind that I was fat.

> # What we focus on, or marinate in our minds, will manifest in our life!

Twelve months later I had gained 50 pounds from the day I began thinking and speaking that I was fat. Now, I was obese, according to the fat index scale or whatever doctors use to tell a person they are obese. I spent the next 30 years at that same weight with that additional 50 pounds of negative thinking.

- Who said something hurtful to you, that you still carry with you today?
- Do you regurgitate negative sentiments or statements about yourself?
- What is the narrative you use to describe yourself?
- Do you speak about yourself in a positive manner?

- Do you believe positive things about yourself?

For nearly 30 ph♥cking years, I carried around an extra 50 pounds of negative images of myself, contributing to low self-esteem, perceived value, and distorted self-image. While I knew I was beautiful on the outside, and in my adult years I carried a positive image according to others, from the very depths of my soul, my view of myself lacked sustained value and worth.

Take your time, you didn't get this way overnight.

I was and am a work in progress, and I am thankful to my many therapists for guiding me on my journey.

Lessons Learned

- We all have trauma.

- We can't fix ourselves alone.

- Church and ministries are not for therapy; they are for spiritual growth.

- Family members can be mentors, too.

- If your children are mentally healthy, seek feedback from them, it's worth it.

- Unpack your bullshit and unpack it often.

- Take your time, you didn't get this way overnight.

You ARE the Most Important Person in the World

Remember when you were in elementary school and the excitement would build for an upcoming Field Day? It was typically towards the end of the school year on a warm sunny day, filled with activities that allowed students to detach from the traditional learning structure and participate in fun and games. I recall my heightened anticipation for participating in the relay races, the potato sack race, the three-legged race, tug-of-war and especially, the 100-yard dash. The teacher would stand at the finish line, whistle tightly held between their lips, prepared to yell the words, "Ready… Set… GO!" I would be in the lineup of students nervously waiting for the word "go" or the sound of the whistle. The anticipation and the excitement I had to run in that 100-yard dash was so innocent and pure. As a kid, I was so unbothered by the dysfunctions in this ph♥cked up world. As a kid, I just wanted to run for fun!

In one of my many moments of deep reflection, I wrote this a few years ago, which caused me to see the 100-yard **dash** very differently than I did as a kid.

The Dash

According to World Data[18], the average age at death in the world is somewhere between 68 years and 73 years old. If each yard represents a year of our lives, by the time you are reading/hearing this, you may already be halfway through your race!

The only things guaranteed in life is that we are born, and we will die. Date of Birth – Date of Death. The only thing a person can control is what happens during the **dash**.

- What legacy will you leave behind?
- What will people say about you when you are gone?

We all leave some kind of mark in this world.

- Will your mark be a big bold one that positively impacts your surroundings?
- Or will it be a small smudge that is barely noticeable?

> # The only thing you can control is what happens during your dash.

Born on Purpose

Each of us was born for a unique purpose - to make and leave our mark in this world. Whether the pregnancy was planned, and your parents eagerly anticipated your arrival, or if you were like me, the result of an unplanned pregnancy, you were still born for a purpose. Think about it, every year, there are more than 2.6 million stillbirths that happen around the world[19]. According to the World Health Organization, there are more than 73 million induced abortions[20] each year. The simple fact that you were born means there was a deliberate intention for you to grace the world with your presence on this earth.

Jeremiah 1:5 (AMP – Amplified Version)

"Before I formed you in the womb, I knew you (and approved of you); before you were born, I consecrated (sanctified or set apart) you."

God knew what He was doing, when He formed you in the womb. Trust Him!

If you consider the above referenced scripture from the Bible, there was a divine plan in the works for you, even before you were formed in your mother's womb. There are millions of sperm cells produced when conception takes place, and the uniqueness of that one sperm cell and that one egg produced the beautiful person you are. There were a lot of competing sperm cells trying to make that connection, but only one made the cut, and that one produced you.

This means that you **were** important enough to be born, and you are equally as important now. You **are** worthy of being here!

If you allow this concept to resonate within your being then you must operate under the premise that you were born on purpose, and it is up to you to find what that purpose is. In **Jeremiah 1:5**, the Word of God says that "He consecrated you or set you apart." We were set apart, unique for our personal calling, and there is an assignment for each one of us to complete.

Identifying your purpose may be met with resistance because we live life based upon our instilled belief systems. Earlier, I shared how our belief system is established based upon our experiences, relationships, and environment. Often, our belief systems are unreliable because they were not established with the full comprehensive awareness of all that we were designed and called to be.

> # Our belief systems can be unreliable.

To broaden our exposure, awareness, and vision, we must explore ourselves deeper than our familial upbringing and step out of what is comfortable into uncomfortable.

I have grown to understand that my purpose in life is to be a maverick. The baby girl who was abandoned at birth and adopted into a ph♥cked up environment (as well-intentioned as it may or may not have been). I am that maverick, the motherless calf, the lone dissenter, an intellectual, one who takes an independent stand. I was created for my assignment to invest my lessons learned in the development and betterment of others, designed to transform my traumatic life experiences into examples for others. My experiences have now become wisdom that I joyfully share with others to help them better navigate this ph♥cked up world in which we live.

> # As an exception, you weren't designed to fit in.

According to Oxford Learner's Dictionaries[21], the definition of **an exception** is:

- A person or thing that is excluded from a general statement or does not follow a rule.

As an exception, you were not designed to fit in. Exception is the foundation of the word exceptional. If there is greatness on the inside of you, just like there is in me, you will be an exception to the rule. You will not fit in. You will feel isolated and misunderstood.

There are millions of people in this world, living life day-by-day, wandering aimlessly and just reacting to whatever comes their way. When you are an exception, a maverick, a motherless calf, that is not how life was designed for you. You were designed to stand out and be exceptional!

Jeremiah 29:11 (NIV)

"For I know the plans I have for you," declares the Lord. "Plans to prosper you and not harm you, plans to give you hope and a future."

You must know that everything you have gone through, every problem, every painful moment, along with every joyful moment, was specifically designed for a purpose far greater than you could ever imagine. I have a tagline at the end of my email signature, and it states, "You are so much more than you think you are."

We all operate with a certain number of blinders, not realizing the significance of who we are to others or how we have left an impression or mark on another person throughout our lives. Just like my friend's wife, who shared with me the impression I left on her more than 35 years ago, we will all leave an indelible mark on this world.

> # You are so much more than you think you are!

When Covid hit the scene, my relationship with the formal church shifted. Rather than tap into the local ministry where I attended, I tapped into an online ministry thousands of miles away from my home. This ministry had consistently provided me with spiritual fuel for more than 25 years in my walk with God. I am now a self-proclaimed "Bedside Baptist," faithfully tuning in each week for spiritual guidance and nourishment for my mind, spirit, and soul. The following are notes I took while listening to a message preached by Bishop T. D. Jakes on 10-23-2023.

- When you are born, you look like your mother and father and when you die, you look like your decisions.

- No one has time, time has you.

- We are born from love.

- We seek love.

- When we die, we are seeking to get love again.

- Remembering is to remind yourself to reconnect back to where you've come from.

- It all starts with our time on earth. Remember it is just a journey.

Bishop T.D. Jakes has been a spiritual mentor to not only me, but millions across the globe, and I have never met him. But for more than 25 years, I have been inspired by his teachings, books, and life lessons that he shares on a variety of platforms and mediums. His spiritual wisdom and teaching come drenched with such functional application to real life situations, and his faithful servantry to ministry has been a guiding light in my life.

Ecclesiastes 9:11 (KJV)

"I returned, and saw under the sun, that the race is not to the swift, nor the battle to the strong, neither yet bread to the wise, nor yet riches to men of understanding, nor yet favour to men of skill; but time and chance happen to them all."

How will you live in the next yard of your dash? Will you be deliberate and intentional in the choices you make? What do you need to do before your race is over? These choices are entirely up to you.

Distractions

Throughout life there will be distractions that interfere with the plans you may have. There will be family members who overly rely on you to get this or that done. You may even take on a much greater role within your family such as a supplemental parental figure for your younger siblings (something I inadvertently required of Laisha). You may be the only person in your family who knows how to make things happen, but that doesn't mean that you are required to do what others want you to do.

My former pastor used to say, "Stay young as long as you can. When you're grown, you're grown for the rest of your life!" A shift occurs in adulthood. We go from being dependent to independent.

While the world mostly says this happens between the ages of seventeen and nineteen, remember that your brain doesn't fully develop until you are in your mid-twenties. I am sure you can agree with me in wanting to forget the actions between late teens and early twenties! At this age, we were not as smart as we thought we were. But, when becoming independent, it is up to us to define the roadmap for our lives.

Do not allow family members and friends to distract you from your passions, purpose, and calling. Remain focused on what's important to you, despite external influences. This journey in life is uniquely yours.

When I understood my assignment or purpose in life is to invest in others, it was very easy for me to become distracted and potentially overwhelmed. Therefore, let me tell you, there is power in the word *no*. If you are like me, someone who likes helping others, saying *no* is empowering! I have found myself saying *yes* when I was screaming on the inside, "Noooooooo!"

When I put myself in the position of saying *yes*, when I really want to say *no*, I am placing undue stress on myself. When others put demands on you, you have the right to make a choice. Remember, just because you can, doesn't mean you should. You can choose to say "no" and not feel guilty about it. This establishes boundaries. You are not responsible for the position other people are in, and you are entitled to say "no."

> # There is power in the word
>
> # "NO."

For me, there have been major distractions I embraced for most of my life. The first one came from my belief that I had to make not just some money, but a lot of money, to provide for my children, to give them a life I didn't have. After dropping out of high school, due to a bad attitude and the birth of Laisha, I formally entered the workplace at the age of sixteen.

In the work environment, we are hired to do a job. We are not hired to invest every waking hour of our days in fulfilling the goals and objectives of our employer - like I did. I allowed my work to be a distraction from my obligation as a parent and not to invest in and raise my children.

I viewed my profession in human resources as doing good for others and walking in my purpose in life. I even felt like I was investing in myself by engaging in a philosophy of lifelong learning: reading books, participating in training events, certifications, professional and spiritual development, every chance I got. However, over the years, I have uncovered that in all that I was doing to invest in myself, much of it was a distraction from the necessary internal work I needed to do. I didn't stop and review the patterns of behavior I displayed at home, at work, and in my intimate relationships.

> # Don't allow your work to distract you from your obligation to be present and engaged as a parent.

I allowed others to spend time with my children when I should have been the one developing their brains, belief systems, and foundations for life. When I decided to give birth, I was unknowingly deciding to no longer live for myself but for another human being. And while we all need money to live, just as we all need oxygen, we cannot allow the pressures of a job to distract us from what should be most important in life. As mentioned earlier, your employer will cut you off as quickly as a tornado rips across an open field and throw you around as if you are useless. Put things in perspective and allow your job to be just that, a job, a means to provide for you and your loved ones. A job enables you to fulfill your purpose in life, which is much more fulfilling than what you do professionally.

I became a natural born giver based upon the underlying feelings of rejection from birth. Some of us who thrive and get intrinsic rewards from doing for others. Regardless of where it stems from, when you are a giver, you will find yourself prioritizing the needs of others before your own. It feels good to help others in need. When I've invested time in another person, I feel like my time on the earth is being well spent. Because this feels good, it is easy to become distracted by doing good for others.

You Time – Investing in Self

In early April 2024, while preparing to file my annual personal and business taxes, I was talking with my accountant. He, like me, enjoys travelling the world to sunny and beautiful destinations. We often comment on each other's social media, expressing jealousy when one or the other has embarked upon a new adventure. We usually connect once or twice a year, and we began our professional relationship almost seven years ago. When we first met, he was the first person to tell me that I needed to start my own business. It is a beautiful space when you have iron sharpening iron. This progressive and independent Black man, a business owner, *saw* this progressive Black woman, who was deficient in a particular area of her life. He chose to invest in me. ❤️

I am grateful for the fellowship, friendship, and business relationship that was born years ago. Our conversations often flow outside of the traditional scope of business, and this is what I appreciate so much about our relationship. So, when he asked me about my recent trip to Thailand, as he is planning a trip there in the fall, I shared with him a few of my experiences and that I wished I had more time to spend with myself on the trip, because I'd filled my itinerary with so much activity.

He then shared with me that he intentionally plans 2-3 trips a year where he can go somewhere by himself, not to explore and participate in what the environment has to offer, but to reflect, process, and regroup. Yes! That is exactly what this most recent adventure missed. I needed a little bit more "me time." We conversed a bit more and transitioned back to addressing business matters. Reflecting on our conversation, I concluded that I must incorporate intentional alone time, to reflect, process, and regroup.

All of us went to some sort of schooling, whether we finished it or not. If you recall, when we were in school, we had quizzes and exams to assess our knowledge of what we were previously taught, and we were graded based upon our responses. At work, we are given quarterly, semi-annual, or annual performance reviews. This is the time our supervisors are to assess our strengths and development opportunities and work with us to develop goals for the upcoming performance period.

> # How can you be the best version of yourself, if you don't take the time to pause, breathe, assess, realign and reset your priorities?

Have you ever considered conducting a personal performance review? What about self-reflection, where you slow down long enough to process and assess what is happening in and around your life? If you are anything like me, life has been life'ing and you haven't. As a Black maverick, I was designed to take a lick and keep it moving. I was designed to navigate obstacles quickly and as my sorority sister says, "You are like a fricking cat, whatever life throws your way, you always land on your feet!" I haven't stopped working, parenting, friending, sistering, or daughtering. I haven't stopped being that intimate partner or trying to save everyone around me. I haven't stopped to just breathe.

How can I bring the best version of myself to any situation if I do not take the time to breathe, regroup, realign my priorities, and reset? I cannot bring forth my best, therefore, I must step back and assess. I must become the most important person in the world, for me to give to others and leave my unique mark on this world.

What my accountant said that evening still resonates within me. If we have embraced and practiced allowing others to assess our effectiveness, why shouldn't we stop and take a moment to assess ourselves?

Turn Trauma into Triumph

I often share with others how I process life's challenges as a blessing and a curse. Born into a feeling of rejection, throughout my life, I mastered how to quicky rebound from ph♥cked up experiences by suppressing my feelings and pushing my way through despite the odds against me. I would give myself three days to process and move on. I felt that if Jesus rose after three days, so could I. While this enabled me to not stay down for very long, it also created an inability to recognize the need to slow down and process my feelings. Ph♥ckIt! I processed and pushed on.

Whether this is healthy or not, I still do not know. Ph♥ckIt! But I do know that I was designed for a purpose, and I am embracing how I deal with obstacles as part of that design. God designed a uniquely qualified woman, full of ph♥cked up experiences, who has chosen to turn trauma into triumph. A Black maverick, created for the purpose of pouring into other people. To lift others, as I climb and navigate through life.

> # Turn trauma into triumph!

To my fellow Black mavericks and Black leaders out there…. Ph♥ckIt! The corporate environment may not have been designed for you, but if you are there, I have an ask of you. When you are blessed with the honor of leading other people, please share your wisdom and experiences with people less knowledgeable than you.

In leadership, it is our duty and obligation to lift others as we climb our own ladder, especially for people who look like us. As you are aware, society is not designed for us to succeed, it was designed to keep us out.

So, when you reach a leadership role, don't be neglectful and fail to provide honest and transparent feedback to those who look to you for leadership. Even if no one ever looked out for you, do better and be better. We need to infuse our community with the wisdom and life experiences of one another. We need to have a soft place to land, to be free, and to express our fears and insecurities. We need to help one another.♥

Remember the excess 50 pounds of weight I gained more than 30 years ago? It has slowly been falling off over the past few years, and I am now physically 50 pounds lighter, and I am still working on shedding the mental weight! God knew what He was doing, before He formed me in the womb. I have been on my journey of transformation, my 50-year transformation to Ph♥ckIt!

When Laisha told me in January 2024 to "let that shit go," that was the beginning of this story. If life is full of our choices that create our own circumstances, we must learn to make new choices. Ph♥ckIt! to my old decision-making process.

Today, I choose to make decisions that empower, enable, and equip me to be the best version of myself. I choose to let all the negative and unnecessary shit go. It has taken me 50 years to get here! My journey of transformation is not over; it has only just begun.

Ph♥ckIt!

I am free to be me.

Lessons Learned

- We are responsible for defining the dash.

- You were born on purpose.

- Distractions will be all around.

- There is power in saying no.

- Choose to assess and invest in yourself.

- Turn trauma into triumph!

Ph❤ckIt! Forgive your parents, they did the best they could with what they had.

Ph❤ckIt! Forgive yourself for your mistakes, you did the best you could with what you had.

Ph❤ckIt! Seek forgiveness from others when you know you have hurt them and do better when you know better.

Ph❤ckIt! Find new friends. You decide who is your inner circle.

Ph❤ckIt! Be single.   Get to know yourself before you enter an intimate relationship.

Ph❤ckIt! Be a Maverick! You weren't designed to fit in.

Ph❤ck Goliath, Katie Kaboom & Mighty Mouse!

Ph❤ckIt! Find a church, a spiritual foundation to strengthen your hope and understanding of God's purpose for your life.

Ph❤ckIt! We all have trauma. Find a therapist or work through your issues. If the first therapist doesn't work out, Ph❤ckIt! find a new one!

Ph❤ck Adversity! **I'm Still Here & Standing Tall!** Ph❤ck Fear!

CAROLE I. WEST

Don't Wait

50 Years
to Say

Wisdom and lessons learned.
Learning to let sh*t go!

References

1. Psychology Today. (2012, August). Developing belief systems about education: It takes a village. Retrieved from https://www.psychologytoday.com/us/blog/psyched/201208/developing-belief-systems-about-education-it-takes-a-village

2. World Health Organization. (n.d.). Child maltreatment. Retrieved from https://www.who.int/news-room/fact-sheets/detail/child-maltreatment

3. Edmondson-Matthews, K. (n.d.). Author page. Plant Glossary. Retrieved from https://plantglossary.com/author/karli-edmondson-matthews/

4. Michigan State University. (2021, August 3). News article. Retrieved from https://socialscience.msu.edu/news-events/news/archives/2021/2021-08-03.html

5. Merriam-Webster. (n.d.). Maverick. In Merriam-Webster.com dictionary. Retrieved from https://www.merriam-webster.com/dictionary/maverick

6. Dictionary.com. (n.d.). Maverick. In Dictionary.com. Retrieved from https://www.dictionary.com/browse/maverick

7. Vocabulary.com. (n.d.). Maverick. In Vocabulary.com. Retrieved from https://www.vocabulary.com/dictionary/maverick

8. DiAngelo, R. (2018). White fragility: Why it's so hard for White people to talk about racism. Beacon Press.

9. 'White Fragility' Author Robin DiAngelo On How To Start Anti-Racist Work : Life Kit : NPR.

10. Katie Ka-Boom. (n.d.). In Animaniacs Wiki. Retrieved from https://animaniacs.fandom.com/wiki/Katie_Ka-Boom

11. (n.d.). Retrieved from
    https://www.bing.com/search?q=why+was+langston+bradley
    +fired+from+dominos

12. Tidesport. (n.d.). Retrieved from
    https://www.tidesport.org/_files/ugd/ac4087_31b60a6a51574
    cbe9b552831c0fcbd3f.pdf

13. Tracy, B. (2010). No excuses: The power of self-discipline.
    Vanguard Press.

14. Wiest, B. (2021). The pivot year. Per Capita Publishing.

15. Maxwell, J. C. (2007). The 21 irrefutable laws of leadership:
    Follow them and people will follow you. Thomas Nelson.

16. Law of action and reaction. (n.d.). In Britannica. Retrieved
    from https://www.britannica.com/science/law-of-action-and-
    reaction

17. Brown, B. (2018). Dare to lead: Brave work. Tough
    conversations. Whole hearts. Random House.

18. World Data. (n.d.). Life expectancy. Retrieved from
    https://www.worlddata.info/life-expectancy.php

19. Aminu, M., & Van den Broek, N. (2019). Stillbirth in low- and
    middle-income countries: Addressing the 'silent epidemic'.
    Published by Oxford University Press on behalf of the Royal
    Society of Tropical Medicine and Hygiene.

20. World Health Organization. (n.d.). Abortion. Retrieved from
    https://www.who.int/news-room/fact-sheets/detail/abortion

21. Oxford Learner's Dictionaries. (n.d.). Exception. Retrieved
    from
    https://www.oxfordlearnersdictionaries.com/us/definition/engl
    ish/exception

About the Author

A seasoned executive with over 30 years of leadership across technology, retail, healthcare, and nonprofit sectors, Carole brings a rare blend of operational excellence, people  strategy, and unapologetic truth-telling into every room she enters. With a degree in Accounting from the University of Arkansas at Pine Bluff and an MBA in Human Resource Management, she has held transformative leadership roles in both Fortune 100 giants and grassroots organizations.

From reviving a $450MM underperforming territory in one of the world's largest retailers, to modernizing HR operations in healthcare and launching a licensed behavioral health facility serving underrepresented communities; Carole doesn't just lead.

She elevates, disrupts, and rebuilds with purpose. But titles aren't what define her.

Her **Audacity** is.

Carole embodies her coaching philosophy, *The Audacity of Being Authentic*, calling leaders to stop just performing and start leading with clarity, presence, and purpose. In a world that rewards fitting in she's learned that it's her calling, as an exception, to stand out.

As a transformational leader, speaker, consultant, and now a published author, Carole's mission is bold and clear: to help high-performing professionals grow from the inside out, with emotional intelligence, strategic insight, and radical self-awareness. Whether she's coaching one-on-one, commanding a stage, or speaking through the pages of her book, Carole invites others to lead with courage, connection, and conviction.

www.divinemomentum.com

www.carolewest.com

www.phuckit.shop

www.ingramcontent.com/pod-product-compliance
Lightning Source LLC
Chambersburg PA
CBHW040854120626
46551CB00001B/14